I0569568

THE
DADDY FILES

How I Survived the Secrets and
Found the Truth that Heals

MELISSA JEAN ROD

©2025 by Melissa Jean Rod

Published by hope*books
2217 Matthews Township Pkwy
Suite D302
Matthews, NC 28105

www.hopebooks.com

hope*books is a division of hope*media

Printed in the United States of America

All rights reserved. Without limiting the rights under copyrights reserved above, no part of this publication may be scanned, uploaded, reproduced, distributed, or transmitted in any form or by any means whatsoever without express prior written permission from both the author and publisher of this book—except in the case of brief quotations embodied in critical articles and reviews.

Thank you for supporting the author's rights.

First paperback edition.
Paperback ISBN: 979-8-89185-258-7
Hardcover ISBN: 979-8-89185-259-4
Ebook ISBN: 979-8-89185-260-0
Library of Congress Number: 2025942717

Scriptures taken from the Holy Bible, New International Version®, NIV®. Copyright © 1973, 1978, 1984, 2011 by Biblica, Inc.™ Used by permission of Zondervan. All rights reserved worldwide. www.zondervan.com The "NIV" and "New International Version" are trademarks registered in the United States Patent and Trademark Office by Biblica, Inc.™

Endorsements

"*The Daddy Files* is a moving account of one daughter's quest to find her biological father—and the unexpected healing she finds in the process. Melissa writes with raw honesty and spiritual insight; this book reminds us that our hope isn't in the answers we chase but in the God who walks with us. If you've ever wrestled with identity, longing, or loss, this story will anchor your heart in the truth: God never lets go."

Kim Mosiman
Author of Reflections of Joy, Wellness Coach, Writing Coach

"You don't just read *The Daddy Files*—you *feel* it. This isn't a story written from the safety of hindsight; it's a testimony told from the trenches of truth, healing, and holy revelation.

I've known Melissa Jean Rod longer than most people know themselves—and I can tell you, this woman doesn't write for applause. She writes because it's how she breathes life into pain, how she honors redemption, and how she reminds every reader that the

Father who sees, knows, and loves us is never late—even when the world feels like it's falling apart.

This book is for every daughter who's ever wondered where she came from, who she really is, and why her story matters. It's for the ones who ache in silence and the ones who carry questions like luggage. If that's you—trust me, you're not alone. Missy's voice will reach into your story like a flashlight and a lifeline.

What she's done here is brave. It's funny in all the right places, gut-wrenching in others, and full of grace from cover to cover. *The Daddy Files* doesn't just share the secrets of a broken beginning—it reveals the beauty of a Father who writes better endings.

If you're holding this book, hold it close. Because what you're really holding is evidence that healing is possible, truth is worth the search, and God—our Abba—is still in the business of turning shattered stories into sacred ones.

Welcome to the file that changed everything."

Dr. Shelley Kemp
Author of *The PIVOT Principle*

Dedication

(Because of course, I have people to thank for this chaos.)

To the best dad a girl could ever ask for, Chuck Hucke, thank you for always being there for me and loving me. For choosing to be my dad. I love you to the moon and back.

To Mom, Renee Hucke, who may not have always understood my path, but whose love has been a constant in my life. Thank you for raising me, and for the love that has helped shape me into who I am today.

To Christina Ann, my sister who so generously shared her dad with me. I've had so much fun with you as my sister. I love you, Dragon Breath.

To my amazing children, Charlie, Spencer, Alyssa, Lynn, Travis, & Cody. God blessed me by placing each of you in my life by different methods. I'm so thankful that I was given the joy of being your mom. I love you the purplest! Thank you for putting up with me while I decided to start writing books at the age of 55.

To my prince charming, my husband, Chuck Rod. Thank you for spoiling me all these years, making my dreams come true, and loving me even when I drive you crazy.

To my ultimate Father, my Abba Father, God. Thank you for every breath You give me, for the love and forgiveness I sometimes take for granted.

Table of Contents

Foreword

It is a rare and beautiful thing to come across a story that not only captures the heart but also invites the reader into deep personal transformation. *The Daddy Files* by Melissa Rod is one such story.

In these pages, you'll journey with Melissa through the raw and powerful process of uncovering her identity, searching for her biological father, and discovering something even greater—a Heavenly Father who never left her side. Her story is both deeply personal and profoundly universal, touching on themes of loss, longing, restoration, and the healing presence of God.

What I found especially impactful were the reflection questions at the end of each chapter. These aren't just afterthoughts—they are invitations. Invitations to pause, reflect, and allow God to work within your own story. I encourage you, dear reader, not to rush through the chapters, but to fully engage with these moments of reflection. Take your time. Journal. Pray. Let the Holy Spirit speak.

The Daddy Files is more than a memoir—it's a ministry tool. Through Melissa's journey, you may find clarity in your own, healing in the places that still ache, and the assurance that your Father in Heaven sees you, knows you, and loves you beyond measure.

This is a book I wholeheartedly recommend, not only for individuals seeking healing but also for ministries walking alongside those on their journey to wholeness.

With expectation for what God will do,

Ava Bates

Certified Christian Counselor / Executive Pastor

The Light Church

Preface

How to Use This Book

(a.k.a. What in the world did I just pick up?)

If you're holding this book in your hands (or scrolling on your screen), you might be wondering what exactly you've stumbled across. Is this a memoir? A detective story? A self-help guide with a little sass and Scripture?

Yes. Yes, to all of the above.

The Daddy Files is my story—but I'm telling it for both of us.

Because maybe, like me, you've gone searching for answers you never thought you'd have to ask. Maybe your past is full of dead ends or missing pieces. Maybe you've been lied to, let down, or left behind. And maybe—just maybe—you've wrestled with who you really are, or wondered if the truth would ever set *you* free.

This book is part emotional rollercoaster, part investigative case file, and part love letter to the Father who never stopped pursuing me.

Each chapter is structured like a case file—because, well, that's what it felt like: evidence gathering, dead-end chasing, breakthroughs, and the slow, sacred process of piecing together a truth I never saw coming. I named this *The Daddy Files* because it felt like I was digging through emotional evidence, trying to find answers to questions I didn't even know I was supposed to ask. At the end of each file, you'll find:

- **Reflection Questions** – To help you process your own story

- **Encouragement** – Because healing is hard, and you don't have to do it alone

- **Writing Prompts** – For when you're ready to go deeper

- **Scripture Anchors** – Truth that never changes, no matter how messy the story gets

You don't have to have all the answers to start reading. You just have to be willing to look. Willing to feel. Willing to let God meet you in the middle of your own search—even if you don't know what exactly you're looking for yet. This is a book for the daughters who were told half the truth—or none at all. For the women still piecing together whom they are beneath the silence. If that's you, welcome.

So, whether you're reading this cover to cover, jumping around to the parts that speak loudest, or simply browsing the field notes like your own spiritual investigation—you're welcome here.

Pull up a chair. Bring your whole heart. Let's open the files together.

Love,
Melissa

A Who's Who

(A cheat sheet so you don't need a flowchart to keep up.)

Allen Slusser – Listed on my birth certificate and the first man I searched for—the "fake father" who came with smooth words, broken promises, and a vanishing act that left more questions than answers. Died in a fire in 1999, taking a whole lot of secrets with him. Not my biological father—but still a part of the story.

Angie Fixico – Elaine's daughter and my DNA-confirmed cousin. We didn't grow up together, but when the truth came out, Angie welcomed me without hesitation. No drama, no doubt—just quiet kindness that helped me feel like I finally belonged.

Betty Ree – My great aunt on Danny's side. With a voice like sweet tea and a heart to match, Betty Ree welcomed me like I'd always belonged. She had stories for days, hugs that healed, and a way of making you feel like kin—even if you'd just met.

Charles (Chuck) Hucke – The man who showed up and never left. My real dad in every way that counts. He adopted me, raised me, and stood tall beside me when I went digging through the past for someone who had disappeared. And when the truth came crashing in—shattering everything I thought I knew—he was still there, holding the pieces. Unshakable. Unconditional. Mine.

Charlie & Spencer – My sons. They held me when the truth hit like a freight train. My living reminders that fatherhood doesn't always follow biology—but love always leaves a mark.

Christina Ann – My little sister by ten years, and the drama to my deadpan. If I'm dry sarcasm and side-eye, she's big feelings and full-volume reactions. Where I keep it cool, she's already crying, yelling, or planning a full Broadway musical about the situation. She was right there with me on the road trip to Oklahoma, riding shotgun as we rolled up on Allen. Christina's been my emotional support hype squad since she could talk—equal parts chaos and loyalty, with a heart bigger than her hair on a humid Texas day. If you ever need someone to ugly cry with you and then threaten your ex with a shoe, she's your girl.

Chuck Rod – My husband, best friend, and partner in every plot twist life threw our way. He came into my life as a single dad doing his best, hired me as a nanny, and ended up being the man I prayed for before I even knew what to ask. He not only loved me but supported me through one of the hardest things I've ever done—searching for the father I never knew. Together we've raised a beautifully blended crew, weathered heartbreak and healing, and proved that sometimes the best stories begin with diapers, chaos, and a whole lot of grace.

Clarence (Grandpa) & Mrs. Hucke – Grandpa, Chuck's dad, and the original strong, silent type. The man barely said a dozen words at a time, but somehow made you feel like you'd been handed ancient wisdom. He treated me like family from the very start—no questions asked, no explanations needed. Mrs. Hucke, Chuck's mom–warmth wasn't her thing, and kindness didn't come easy—but she was part of the package. She wasn't exactly warm or welcoming—more like polite with a side of frost. I learned how to navigate those chilly waters with grace and grit.

Coach – Private investigator and father of my boss. He found Allen for me the second time around. Proved that sometimes the biggest answers come from small-town loyalty and a good Rolodex

Danny Demings – My biological father, confirmed through DNA and a God-given dream. Deceased. Never met him in life, but God introduced us in a dream that felt more real than anything. His name didn't show up on a certificate—but it was always written in my DNA.

David Demings – Danny's brother, also deceased. Appeared in the same dream with Danny before I even knew who they were. Heaven had a head start on the case.

David Smith – My mom's younger brother and one of my earliest father figures. He taught me to ride a bike, made me laugh, and had a heart bigger than Texas. Quick with a joke and never one to take life too seriously, he helped fill the gap when my dad was missing— without ever making a big deal about it.

Dorothy Clark Slusser – Allen's mother. A nurse with a complicated past, Dorothy battled addiction and died tragically in 1964—murdered in her own home. I never knew her, but her story cast a long shadow. She was a woman marked by pain, and though her life ended before mine began, the ripples of her choices reached all the way to me.

Elaine Blanton – Danny's sister and my aunt. She welcomed me like I'd always belonged. Our first visit was on my birthday, and it changed everything.

Eric – Johnny's son and my almost-brother for a hot minute. For a brief, hopeful stretch, I thought we shared DNA. We didn't— but that didn't stop him from being kind, gracious, and generous with his story. Proof that, sometimes, even false leads can bring real connection.

Granny & Granddaddy Smith – The heart and soul of my childhood. Granny ruled the kitchen with a mixing spoon and a raised eyebrow—her red velvet cake could fix anything except maybe a broken heart (but she'd try anyway). Granddaddy was my first hero, the man in the orange recliner who made me feel safe just by being there. He taught me how to appreciate the quiet and how a lap could be the safest place in the world. Together, they filled my life with love, laughter, and a kind of everyday magic you don't realize is extraordinary until you're grown.

Johnny & Mason – Dead ends. Men I thought could be my father during the search. Their short appearances gave me hope, and their exits gave me grit.

Lola Slusser – Allen's grandmother and the unexpected bright spot in a very murky mess. She welcomed me into her home and heart like she'd been waiting for me all along—with coffee brewing, stories ready, and a hug that could make the world feel right again. Deeply faithful and fiercely kind, she read her Bible every morning and treated me like family before the rest of them even made eye contact. In a moment when I could've felt like an outsider, Lola made sure I felt seen, loved, and completely at home.

Renee Smith Hucke – My mother. Complicated. Protective. Guarded. Carried her own secrets for decades. Her denials delayed the truth, but her choices shaped the search.

Confidentiality Notice (a.k.a. A Quick Word from the Investigator's Desk)

Some names in this file have been changed—not to protect the guilty (although, you never know ...)—but to honor privacy, preserve dignity, or simply avoid awkward holiday gatherings.

People are complicated. Memories are tender. Lawsuits are expensive. If you think you recognize someone—you might be right. Or maybe you've just watched too many true crime shows. Either way, the stories are true, the feelings are real, and the healing is holy.

Proceed accordingly.

Prologue: Who Am I?

*(Where I set the stage, and you realize you're
in for one heck of a story.)*

*"And we know that in all things God works for the good of those
who love him, who have been called according to his purpose."*
— **Romans 8:28**

You might be wondering: why read a memoir from someone you've never heard of? Let me tell you—because this isn't just my story. It's a story about loss, love, forgiveness, and finding hope in the unexpected.

I'm not famous. I'm just an everyday Stay-at-Home Mom—or SAHM, as the acronym goes. My husband and his brothers love to joke about my easy life of soaps and bonbons, but let me tell you, raising kids is no small feat. These days, I just laugh along and tell them the champagne made it sublime.

Maybe you picked up this book because you're curious. Or maybe, like me, you've felt lost—searching for answers, stumbling through life's muck, and wondering if anyone really understands how you feel. I get it. I've been there. Life has a way of throwing curveballs that knock the wind right out of us, leaving us questioning who we are, where we belong, and how we're supposed to move forward.

And me? I didn't always have the answers. I still don't. But what I've learned along the way—through the hurt, the loss, and the unexpected twists—is worth sharing. My journey taught me about forgiveness, about finding hope in the hardest places, and about trusting God even when life doesn't make sense.

Maybe you're just curious about this rambling blonde mom from Texas. Whatever brought you here, I pray that God will use this in your life.

How do you know who you'll become? How do you know what will truly matter to you later—whether that later is a week, a month, a year, or even decades down the road? When you're a kid, growing up seems like the ultimate dream. You think life will magically get easier, simpler, better. Spoiler alert: it doesn't.

Not always, anyway.

It's not that life is bad—it's just different. Harder. More complicated. Full of decisions you don't always see coming.

Some choices seem small, harmless, almost laughably insignificant at the time. But life has a way of showing you just how big those small choices can be. They're like tiny pebbles dropped into a pond, sending ripples outward. Sometimes, those ripples turn into waves, pushing you down paths you never anticipated. Looking back, you see how those little moments shifted everything.

As a teenager, I was so sure of myself. I thought I knew right from wrong, black from white. I thought I had the world all figured out.

And of course, I didn't.

Hindsight is humbling that way.

Now, when I glance in the rearview mirror of time, I see that younger version of me so clearly—a girl full of ideals and absolutes, convinced she had all the answers.

In some ways, I miss her.

I miss her hope and her belief that love could conquer anything. I miss her naivete, even when it was wrong—because it came with unshakable dreams and the promise of the whole world ahead of her.

But life has a way of teaching you, doesn't it?

Innocence fades. And in its place comes wisdom ... experience ... compassion.

I still believe in right and wrong, in black and white, but now? I see the gray more clearly. I understand it better, and I feel it more deeply.

And while that younger version of me might've judged others harshly, the me of today knows that compassion carries far more weight than judgment ever could.

If I had uncovered the truth about my conception as a teenager, I don't think I would have handled it well at all.

I believed everything my mother ever told me.

Remember how I said I was naive?

Boy, was I.

It never even crossed my mind to question her. I never imagined she would lie to me—especially about something as important as who my father was.

Really, why would she?

Why would anyone?

Looking back now, I can see how unprepared that younger version of me would have been.

If I'd discovered the truth 30 or 40 years ago, I wouldn't be the person I am today. I know that much for certain.

The younger me would have been consumed by hurt and anger, unable to comprehend how or why a mother could make that choice.

Even now, I struggle to decide—would it have hurt more back then, or does it cut deeper knowing the truth now?

What I do know is this: I was better equipped to handle it now than I ever would have been then.

Still, the pain is real.

I missed out on so much because of the secret my mom kept all those years.

Who my father truly was—the truth of my own identity—was hidden from me. I lived a lie.

Not one of my choosing.

Not one I even knew about.

But a lie, nonetheless.

And it wasn't just a lie about someone else—it was a lie that cut to the core of who I believed I was.

It shaped the choices and decisions I made throughout my life.

How do you forgive someone for that?

How do you move forward after such a life-altering discovery?

The answer is simple but not easy: one step at a time. In fact, sometimes it is minute by minute.

Forgiveness is a process, and it doesn't come without setbacks. You'll think, *I've got this!* You'll feel a wave of relief, convinced the pain has finally loosened its grip.

And then—out of nowhere—it will slam into you again.

The hurt. The sorrow. The loss.

But there will also be days of peace. Days when the pain has faded, when the sorrow isn't as heavy, when life feels good again.

You may not see them yet. You may still be sitting in the ache, wondering if the weight will ever lift. But healing has a quiet way of sneaking in—through laughter you didn't expect, a sunset that stops you in your tracks, or a moment when you realize you're breathing a little easier. It won't happen all at once, but little by little, light finds its way back in.

Those days will come.

Don't give up. Keep going. Keep forgiving, even when it feels impossible.

Not for the person you're forgiving, but for yourself.

Because if you don't—if you let anger and bitterness, take root—it will only eat away at you.

It will rob you of even more than you've already lost.

Forgiveness doesn't erase the pain, but it does loosen its hold.

And in that space, healing begins.

At the heart of my journey, I've learned that healing and forgiveness are only possible with God's guidance.

And so, I prayed.

> *Father, please guide me as I write this. Let me stay out of Your way so that Your words are clearly heard, and Your love is felt. Thank You for always being there, every step of the way. Amen.*

This is the story of what I lost, what I found, and the Father who walked with me through it all.

Field Notes:
Evidence for Healing

Identity isn't found in the stories others tell us; it's found in the One who created us.

REFLECTION QUESTIONS

- How do you usually describe your life story to others?
- In what ways has your identity been shaped by missing pieces or unanswered questions?
- Have you ever had to reframe your story when the truth didn't match the version you were told?

ENCOURAGEMENT

You are not just the product of your past—you're the continuation of a story still being written. Even if the pages before felt torn or scribbled with secrets, God is the Author who brings clarity from chaos and beauty from brokenness. Your identity isn't lost—it's waiting to be uncovered, one truth at a time.

God isn't afraid of your questions. He's not thrown off by your mess. He already knows the whole story—and He's still calling you His.

WRITING PROMPT

Start a "case file" on yourself. Write a brief summary of who you are—not the roles you play, but who you are deep down. Include your hopes, questions, and the mysteries you're still trying to solve.

SCRIPTURE ANCHOR

"Before I formed you in the womb I knew you, before you were born I set you apart..."

— **Jeremiah 1:5**

PRAYER

God, I come to You with pieces of a story that sometimes feel scattered, confusing, or incomplete. Help me trust that You are not only present in the unknowns—but that You're also guiding me toward truth and healing. Show me who I am through Your eyes and anchor my identity in Your love. Amen.

Fatherless Dreams In Search of a Father: Longing for Love and Belonging

*"Though my father and mother forsake me,
the Lord will receive me."*
– Psalm 27:10

Hello and welcome to my little corner of the world. Buckle up, because I've got a wild tale to share with you. Fair warning: it might get a little confusing at times, so grab your favorite drink (tea, coffee, or something stronger—I'm not judging), maybe a notepad and a pen if you're the note-taking type. Pull up a chair, get comfy, and let me introduce you to my drama. Trust me, it's worth sticking around for.

To really understand my story, we have to start where every story does: childhood. I was like every other little girl in most ways—except for one glaring difference: no dad in the picture. I had a mom who loved me, grandparents who spoiled me rotten, and an aunt and uncles who doubled as siblings. Wait—scratch that. That's not like every other little girl. But it was my world. It was all I knew.

Until I started school and got to know other kids, I didn't realize it wasn't exactly the norm. Well, that and what I saw on TV—but that's a whole other thing. I mean, I was born in the late '60s, so by the time I was watching TV in the '70s, it was a different ball game altogether.

We all grew up in our own kinds of families, didn't we? Some were picture-perfect, others a little messy. But on TV in the '70s? Families came in every flavor imaginable. Do you remember *The Partridge Family*? *The Munsters*? *The Brady Bunch*? *Bewitched*? Those shows painted these wonderfully quirky, colorful pictures of what 'family' could look like. None of them were traditional, and neither was mine.

And those shows? They didn't just keep me entertained—they shaped my humor. Shows like *The Munsters* and *The Addams Family* taught me to find the funny in life's oddities. Let me tell you, that's a skill that's saved my sanity more times than I can count!

Growing up, I wanted what every little kid wants—a daddy. My own daddy. Grandaddy and my uncles were wonderful—they taught me to fish, tied the laces on my first sneakers, and cheered when I wobbled on my bike without training wheels. But they weren't the dad I longed for. I wanted what my friends had—a father who picked me up from school, twirled me around, and called me his little girl. Every time I saw another child with their dad, that longing grew sharper, like a splinter I couldn't pull out.

I loved my family, and honestly, except for not having a dad of my own, life was good. How could it not be? I was the Golden Child. The first grandchild. The first niece. Spoiled ROTTEN. I'll admit it—I was the favorite. Still am. (That's an ongoing joke in my mom's family. We all claim to be Granny's favorite, but let's be real. It's me. Don't tell the others.)

Despite all the love and attention I got from my family, there was still a void—a shadow I couldn't ignore. I felt the absence of a father. Grandaddy was devoted, but he wasn't my dad. And as I watched other kids with their fathers, I couldn't shake the feeling that I was missing something.

Granny's kitchen was the heart of our home, filled with the smells of love and a dash of mischief. The sweet, rich scent of her red velvet cake batter would fill the air, a smell so decadent it felt like an event all on its own. I'd stand on a chair pulled up to the counter, practically vibrating with excitement as I waited for her to hand me the beaters.

"Here you go, Missy," she'd say with a knowing smile, passing me the batter-covered beaters. I'd lick every bit of that ruby-red magic off, savoring the taste of vanilla, cocoa, and sugar. But by the time I was done, my fingers were stained bright red—a mark of my impatience as I scraped every last drop from the bowl and beaters.

Then there was the icing. Granny never used cream cheese frosting for her red velvet cakes—not her style. No, she made the traditional cooked icing, a silky, sweet concoction whipped to perfection. And while I loved licking the batter, sneaking fingerfuls of that divine frosting was an experience all its own.

Granny always pretended to scold me when she caught me dipping my fingers into the frosting bowl. "Missy Jean, you'll eat it all before it gets on the cake!" she'd laugh, shaking her head, but the twinkle in her eye let me know she didn't mind one bit.

Her kitchen wasn't just a place for baking—it was a sanctuary. A place where I felt safe, loved, and whole. For a little girl yearning for a father, those moments in Granny's kitchen were my refuge.

Granddaddy and my uncles did their best to stand in that gap. They taught me how to do the little things kids are supposed to learn—but also made sure I knew I was loved. They made me laugh, loved me fiercely, and protected me in ways I couldn't appreciate back then. Because all I could see was what I didn't have. I missed the ways God had placed these incredible men in my life. All I saw was the empty chair. As a young child, you notice things around you, but you don't fully grasp their meaning. You see parts of situations— fragments of conversations or glimpses of expressions—but without understanding the full story. You take in just a piece of it, sometimes only noticing how it feels rather than what it means.

Growing up, the questions about my dad were always there, lingering in the background like an unfinished story. But I could never have imagined how deeply those questions would shape my life—or how God would use them to draw me closer to Him.

As a child, I longed for a father to fill the empty space in my life, to answer the "why's" that kept me awake at night. I couldn't have known then that God was already working, already weaving a story so much greater than the one I was dreaming of.

Mom wasn't sure if God was real, but she hoped. She prayed that God would send a man into her life who would love me as much as he loved her. She was only 20 years old—young, scared, and trying to figure it all out. Divorced and with a small baby, she had moved back to her childhood home, surrounded by her parents and siblings. She wanted more for me and never stopped asking for it. Night after night, she poured her heart out to a God she wasn't even sure existed.

"If You're real," she'd pray, "please send someone who will love Missy as much as he loves me." She didn't have all the answers, but she held onto hope—hope that someone, somewhere, was listening and would answer her prayers.

What I didn't realize back then was that my search wasn't just about finding my father. It was about finding myself, and, as I would come to learn, finding God's plan for me all along.

Looking back, I see that while I was searching for a father, God was already there—whispering to my heart that I was never truly alone. He was showing me that family is not just who's there but who's willing to stay and love you, no matter what.

Even though I didn't understand it yet, God's love was the thread that tied it all together.

Field Notes:
Evidence for Healing

The longing for a father's love points us to the deeper truth: we were made for a relationship with God.

REFLECTION QUESTIONS

- Have you ever longed for something so deeply it felt like part of your identity?

- What early desires or unmet needs still echo in your adult life?

- How has your view of "family" been shaped by what you lacked or what you gained?

ENCOURAGEMENT

Longing is not a weakness; it's a window into the deeper parts of who you are. God sees every tear, every "why not me," every quiet wish you tucked away as a child. He doesn't dismiss those dreams. Instead, He repurposes them, building something even stronger on the very ground where your heart once broke. The longing in your heart was never unnoticed. He sees it. *He sees you*. He heard every prayer, even the ones you didn't know how to pray.

WRITING PROMPT

Think back to yourself as a child. What did you want more than anything? Write a letter from your current self to that younger version of you. Speak to her with truth, comfort, and the kind of love she didn't know how to ask for.

SCRIPTURE ANCHOR

"A father of the fatherless, a defender of widows, is God in His holy dwelling. God sets the lonely in families ..." – **Psalm 68:5-6a**

PRAYER

Father God, thank You for seeing the places in my life where something—or someone—was missing. Thank You for the people You sent to love me in those spaces, even when I didn't recognize it as Your provision. Heal the old wounds, Lord, and remind me that I've never been truly alone. You have always been writing my story, and I trust You with the rest of it. Amen.

CASE FILE #002

A Broken Beginning

"As for me, I call to God, and
the LORD saves me."
– Psalm 55:16

A t 19 years old, my mom was living in Glasgow, Montana—about as far removed from her Gulf Coast Texas roots as you could get. With a small-town heart and a whole lot of grit, she had landed near an Air Force base, learning to spread her wings and do life on her own.

That's where she met Allen Slusser—at a gas station of all places. She pulled in to fill up, and Allen, working part-time off base, stepped in like a scene out of an old movie. He pumped her gas, probably with a wink and a smile, and just like that, their story began. (What can I say? Romance in the '60s was built on leaded gasoline and good timing.)

They hit it off—young, impulsive, and full of that wild spark that makes you believe anything's possible. According to Mom, he had charm, confidence, and just enough mystery to make her believe this might be something. And apparently, it was—because before long, I was on the way.

Now, let's pause for a reality check: it was the middle of the Vietnam War. They were young, unmarried, emotions were high, and the future was uncertain. Things were rocky from the start. My mom—still just a teenager herself—found herself pregnant in a new town, far from home. She seriously considered placing me for adoption. She even had a family picked out—a local couple ready to raise the baby she wasn't sure she could keep.

But Allen had other plans. Somewhere between fear and responsibility—or maybe pride and pressure—he decided they'd get married and "make a go of it." So, at five months pregnant, Mom and Allen went to a Justice of the Peace and tied the knot.

It wasn't exactly a fairytale wedding—unless your fairy tale includes go-go boots, a pink mini dress, and a very pregnant walk to the courthouse. No big, white dress with a mile-long train sweeping the floor. No fancy cake with their names piped in frosting swirls. Just a courthouse, a shaky signature, a promise. Two people betting everything they had on a "happily ever after" they barely understood—too young to know what forever really meant.

> (*Quick side note: Years later, I'd learn that the ink wasn't even dry on Allen's divorce from his first wife before marrying my mom. Awkward.*)

Shortly after their marriage, they moved to Texas. Allen was stationed at Lackland Air Force Base in San Antonio for a short stint before receiving new orders on the East Coast.

They didn't stay long in Texas—but it was long enough to mark a new chapter: my arrival.

But the "happily ever after" never showed up. The first few months as a family of three were rough. Really rough.

This wasn't a Hallmark movie setup. There were no cozy endings, no magical fixes. He drank. He raged. He could be cruel. What began as stress and arguments turned into something darker. The fights grew more intense. The tension more dangerous. The line between emotional pain and physical danger was crossed.

I was just a baby, lying in my crib, when the world cracked open.

I had been asleep—the deep, heavy kind of sleep only babies know—until something, some noise, jolted me awake.

I don't know what Mom and Allen were doing before that moment. Laughing, fighting, sitting in heavy silence. I'll never know. I just know that when I started to cry, everything exploded.

Mom moved toward me—I can still picture it in my mind, the way a mother moves when her child cries, instinct pulling her faster than thought. But Allen wouldn't let her.

He shoved her once.

Hard enough that she stumbled back.

She tried again—pushing past him, reaching for me.

And this time, he hit her.

I don't remember the sound of his hand, but I can imagine it: sharp, ugly, echoing off the walls that were supposed to be our home. Our safe place.

I don't remember the words they screamed at each other—if there were words at all. But I know fear has a sound, and it's louder than anything else.

In my crib, I must have screamed too. Not understanding. Not knowing why the world suddenly felt wrong—only knowing that it did.

And that was the moment everything changed.

I don't know how long it lasted—the shoving, the shouting, the fear thick in the air.

But I know this: something shifted in her that night.

Maybe it was the way he raised his hand again. Maybe it was the sound of my cries growing hoarse. Maybe it was the cold, sharp clarity that comes when you realize you have nothing left to lose.

Whatever it was, Mom made a choice. She didn't wait for things to get better. She didn't wait for an apology. She didn't wait for him to calm down.

She grabbed me—screaming, shaking, alive—from the crib.

Mom did the bravest thing a young mother could do: She picked up the phone and called her parents—shaking, crying, done. "Come get Missy and me," she said.

I can't imagine the fear she must have felt sitting in a dim room with a tiny baby, bruised and broken, picking up that phone. But she did it.

And Granddaddy didn't hesitate.

He grabbed the keys to the family station wagon and came for us.

He drove all night from Texas to Charleston, South Carolina. When he arrived, they packed up everything we owned in a U-Haul, loaded us into the car, and made the long drive back to Texas. Back home. Back where we'd be safe. Back where we'd be loved.

I don't remember the drive back to Texas. But I've often wondered: Did the sound of the wheels on the highway soothe me? Did I feel the tension in Mom's arms as she held me tighter that night?

Now, as a mom myself, I understand more than ever what real bravery looks like. It's not flashy. It's not loud. It's a shaking hand dialing a phone. It's a battered heart refusing to give up.

It's a mother, bruised but unbroken, choosing to fight for her child's future even when she's terrified.

Because of her courage, I got the chance to live a different story. And even though my earliest chapter was full of brokenness, it was also marked by something stronger:

A mother's love that refused to leave me behind.

It was 1969, and the world felt upside down.

I'd just entered it.

Field Notes:
Evidence for Healing

Our broken starting points do not define our final destinations.

REFLECTION QUESTIONS

- Have you ever seen someone you love caught in a relationship that was breaking them down instead of building them up?

- What does safety mean to you—and how has that changed throughout your life?

- Are there parts of your story that began in pain but led you somewhere stronger?

ENCOURAGEMENT

You may not remember your earliest wounds, but God does. He sees the pain you couldn't name and the fear you couldn't voice. And He's been rescuing you ever since. The beginning of your story doesn't define the end. In fact, it may just be the backdrop to something far more beautiful.

WRITING PROMPT

Write about a time someone made a hard decision to protect you— or when you had to protect someone else. What did it cost? What did it teach you about courage?

SCRIPTURE ANCHOR

"The LORD is close to the brokenhearted and saves those who are crushed in spirit."

— Psalm 34:18

PRAYER

Lord, thank You for being present in every part of my story—even the broken beginnings. Help me to trust that You are writing something redemptive, even when the start was messy. Give me eyes to see the protection You've provided and the courage it took for those who stepped in when I couldn't help myself. Amen.

A Father's Love

"I will be a Father to you, and you will be my sons and daughters, says the Lord Almighty."
– 2 Corinthians 6:18

God is an amazing Father to us. He loves us unconditionally—a truth I've clung to during my search for love and belonging. His promise in 2 Corinthians 6:18 isn't just a comforting thought—it's a reality I've seen reflected in my life, through the father He sent me and the lessons I've learned about His love.

He wants the best for us. He waits for us to come to Him and share our day—our hurts, our successes, our struggles. Like any loving father, He listens. He waits. And He loves us unconditionally. He loves us so much that He sent Jesus—His Son, our Brother—to die for us, so that we might truly live.

This promise isn't just words on a page; it's the heartbeat of who God is. He's not a distant deity. He's our Father—ready to welcome, guide, and hold us close no matter where we've been or what we've done.

As much as I longed for my biological father, God knew what I needed most. He sent me Dad—a man who would reflect His love in ways I couldn't fully appreciate until much later.

It was March 1975. Mom might not have been sure if there was really a God, but He answered her prayer. She prayed that if God was real, He would send someone who would love me—Missy—as much as he loved her. And He did. I was so desperate for a father's love. I wanted a daddy. I had a hole that needed to be filled. And God sent me a daddy. Enter my dad, Chuck Hucke.

From their first date, Dad made sure that I was always included. Mom went to a local bar one night with a girlfriend. It was one of their regular spots, where they knew everyone—including the bartender and waitress. The plan was simple: have a fun girls' night and invite their friends to Mom's birthday party that weekend. Meanwhile, Chuck Hucke was there, nursing a toothache. He'd had a tooth pulled earlier that day and decided to skip the prescription meds in favor of a drink. This is funny for so many reasons—mainly because Dad's never been much of a drinker. One beer, and he's out for the count.

Mom's friend introduced them and invited Chuck Hucke to the party. Sure enough, Chuck showed up, and he didn't come empty-handed. He brought magic tricks. Lots of them. Turns out, he was great at illusions and had everyone—me and the neighborhood kids especially—completely mesmerized.

I think I fell in love with him that day. Mom? Well, she took a little bit longer.

"Our" first date was ... memorable, to say the least. Knowing Mom, I'm honestly a little surprised she agreed to a second one!

Somehow, Chuck persuaded her to go skating. She warned him she wasn't good, and I had never been before. I was six at the time. He assured her that he wasn't very proficient either—that we'd all help each other along.

That's how we found ourselves at a skating rink straight out of a '70s fever dream—dark walls with neon stripes, a glittering disco ball spinning overhead, and the unmistakable scent of popcorn, rubber wheels, and floor polish in the air. The whole place pulsed with the sound of a funky bassline as a DJ's voice echoed over the speakers: *"All skate! Everybody, all skate!"*

The rink was surrounded by what I later learned was called the *panic rail*—a smooth wooden railing that kids like me (and, I suspected, plenty of nervous adults) clung to for dear life. I remember watching seasoned skaters zoom by effortlessly, weaving through the clumsy ones like they were born on wheels, while others stumbled, grabbed at thin air, and crashed into the floor with a thud.

Mom, gripping Chuck's hand a little tighter than necessary, looked like she was rethinking her life choices. I, on the other hand, was wide-eyed, taking it all in—the flashing lights, the whir of wheels against the floor, the occasional shriek of someone wiping out, and the smell of nacho cheese mingling with sweat and old leather skates.

It didn't take long for me to realize that when Chuck said he "wasn't very proficient," he was being wildly optimistic.

So off we went, stumbling, falling, and laughing like raving lunatics.

Holding hands, with Chuck in the middle, we shuffled along like a wobbly three-legged race on wheels. The *panic rail* was never far from reach, and we used it liberally, gripping it for balance when our legs decided to do their own thing—which was often. The rink's speakers blasted *Earth, Wind & Fire* while skaters breezed past us with that effortless, almost smug, confidence that only comes from having spent far too many Friday nights under the disco ball.

After a few shaky laps, we had learned two important things: If one of us lost balance, the other two were going down like dominoes and second, we did not, in fact, want to go down like dominoes.

So, when Chuck wobbled again—arms flailing, knees buckling—Mom and I made a split-second decision, born out of pure self-preservation. We dropped his hands like hot potatoes.

We braced ourselves, ready to watch him hit the deck. It was basic physics, right? One second, he was teetering, about to eat the floor, and the next ...

Well.

The next second, he was *gone*.

Not sprawled out on the ground like we expected. No, not even close.

Chuck, dear sweet *uncoordinated* Chuck, caught his balance, straightened up, and then—just to add insult to injury—took off across the rink like he was auditioning for *Xanadu*.

With a grin as wide as Texas, he spun around and started skating *backward*, hands behind his back, looking at us like he'd been waiting all night for this moment.

"Oh, did I forget to mention?" he called out, gliding effortlessly. "I used to work at a skating rink."

Mom and I just stood there, jaws on the floor, struggling to process this betrayal.

I mean, this man had *lied* to us. Boldly. Straight-faced. "Not very proficient," my foot.

As for me? That was it. I was hooked.

I hate to admit that I didn't appreciate him like I should have. It took too many years before I realized what a wonderful father God had given me.

Chuck Hucke wasn't just my mother's husband. He wasn't just a man who stepped into our lives. He was *there*—always there. Steady, unwavering, and loving me in a way I didn't even recognize as the rare gift it was.

He loved me like I was his own ... and in his eyes, I was.

He never treated me any differently than his other daughters. Never hesitated to include me, to claim me, to be *mine*. I was his little girl, just as much as if we had shared the same blood.

But I didn't see it. I didn't understand what a treasure that was.

Because I wanted what wasn't there.

I wanted my birth father.

I wanted my questions answered.

I wanted to know *why*.

What was wrong with me that my birth father didn't want me?

I couldn't see past that aching, unanswered void, that desperate need to belong to *him*—the man I'd never known. And in my blindness, I missed what was right in front of me.

I missed the love of the man who *did* choose me.

The man who *stayed*.

Chuck took after his father. Clarence Hucke was *something else*. I didn't know what to expect when I met him and Mrs. Hucke for the first time, but I knew this: these were the people who would one day be my grandparents. And I wanted so badly for them to love me.

It was late when we left Channelview, the kind of deep Texas night where the heat still clings to the air even after the sun goes down. The hum of the highway filled the silence between our words as Mom, Chuck, and I made the long drive to Alexandria, Louisiana. I sat in the backseat, my fingers tracing patterns on the window, the glass cool against my fingertips. Every now and then, I'd catch Chuck's reflection in the rearview mirror—his easygoing expression, the slight smile playing on his lips. He was excited to see his folks.

Me? I was nervous.

When we finally pulled into the driveway of their modest home, I could barely sit still. My stomach twisted with anticipation as Chuck put the car in park and stretched, letting out a sigh like he was already home. But I wasn't. Not yet.

The porch light flickered, casting a warm glow over the front steps. Chuck opened the door, stepping inside like he belonged there—because he did. I followed closely behind, my small hand wrapped around my mother's fingers, though I wasn't sure if I was holding on to her for comfort or if she was holding on to *me*.

Inside, the house smelled like something old and familiar—like coffee, faint cigarette smoke, and the lingering scent of a home-cooked meal. The kind of place where time moved a little slower.

Then she appeared.

His mom, Mrs. Hucke.

She wasn't unkind at first, at least not outwardly. Chuck hugged her like a son who had missed his mother, his voice warm with affection as he introduced me. "Mom, this is Melissa."

She nodded, offering me a brief glance before shifting her focus back to him. "Long drive?"

"Yeah, but we made good time," he said, smiling as he set the suitcase down by the door.

Then, just like that, he was gone—off to grab more bags, stepping outside with a cigarette dangling between his fingers.

And that's when it happened.

The air in the room seemed to shift. Mrs. Hucke turned, her eyes settling on me for the first real time, sizing me up. My heart pounded in my chest as I stood there, still gripping my mother's hand, desperate for warmth, for kindness, for some sign that I belonged.

But instead, she looked down at me—a seven-year-old little girl who just wanted to be loved—and said, in a voice cold and certain, *"You're not April. You're not kin, and you never will be."*

Then, just like that, she turned and walked into the kitchen, leaving me standing there, my breath caught in my throat, and my mother silent beside me.

I never told Chuck.

He loved his mom. And because I loved *him*, I called her Grandma. Because I knew that would make him happy.

Now, *Grandpa*? Grandpa was the total opposite.

Clarence Hucke was a gift that night to a confused and hurting little girl.

After what had happened with Mrs. Hucke, I had curled up on the couch, pulling my knees to my chest, trying to make myself small. I didn't cry—I wouldn't let myself—but there was an ache deep in my chest, the kind that came from feeling unwanted. The kind that came from hearing words meant to push you away.

The house was dim, the warm glow of a single lamp casting soft shadows on the walls. The smell of coffee lingered in the air, mixing with the scent of cigarette smoke clinging to the furniture, but I barely noticed. My stomach was still knotted, my thoughts spinning. Would he be like *her*? Would he see me as an outsider, too?

Then the front door opened.

The night air rushed in as boots scuffed against the entryway. The man who stepped inside was big—not just in size, but in presence. His uniform was wrinkled from a long shift, his silver hair slightly disheveled, and his face ... his face told a story all its own. Deep wrinkles carved into his skin like the lines of a well-worn map, each one a mark of the years he had worked, lived, and loved. But his eyes—his eyes were kind.

In one hand, he held a chocolate cake, the kind with thick, rich frosting that looked almost too good to be real. In the other, a stuffed animal—a soft, soon to be well-loved bear with a lopsided bow around its neck.

And then, he spoke.

"Where is my granddaughter, Missy?"

I sat up, blinking in surprise. Had I heard that right?

Before I could even find my voice, he was already moving, setting the cake down, kneeling in front of me, his big hands reaching out as if I had always belonged there. Up close, I could see the deep creases in his skin even more clearly, the ones that framed his smile, the ones around his eyes that told me he had spent a lifetime laughing, even through the hard times.

And then he pulled me into his arms.

"I am so happy that you will be my granddaughter," he said, his voice warm and certain, like it was the most natural thing in the world.

And just like that, the ache in my chest loosened.

That was all I needed.

I was blessed by the men in that family. Mrs. Hucke passed away when I was 13 years old. Grandpa, on the other hand, lived until I was 29. He passed away in May 1997. I gave birth to Spencer, my firstborn, in June that same year. It's always made me sad that, except for my step-son, Charlie, who doesn't remember him, my children never got to meet that wonderful man.

Thanks to Dad and Grandpa Hucke, I knew what unconditional love was. I was loved by men who adopted me into their family, just like God does for us when He sent Jesus so we could be adopted into His heavenly family. He loves us so much. It's amazing when you think about it.

> No matter what we do, Jesus loves us and forgives us if we just ask. *"See what great love the Father has lavished on us, that we should be called children of God! And that is what we are!"*
>
> **(1 John 3:1a)**

I've often reflected on how God is a Father who welcomes us into His family—not out of obligation, but out of love. No matter where we've been, what we've done, or how lost we may feel, He calls us His own. He doesn't just tolerate us—He chooses us. That truth became even more real to me through my own adoption story. I remember the mix of emotions that day: the uncertainty of what was ahead, the fear of stepping into something new, and the quiet hope that I was finally part of something permanent. But more than anything, I remember the overwhelming presence of love.

Adoption isn't just a legal process; it's a declaration of belonging. It's someone looking at you and saying, "You are mine. No conditions. No doubts." That's exactly what God does for us. He doesn't hesitate. He doesn't second-guess. He simply welcomes us in, giving us a name, a place, and a love that can never be undone

It started with a phone call.

It was a Saturday morning, and I was doing what any kid would do—watching cartoons and eating a Pop-Tart. The phone rang, and

Mom called me into the room. *"Missy,"* she said, *"Allen's on the phone. He wants to talk to you."*

Allen.

The man I had always thought of as my father, but who had never been a part of my life. He was the man we had to track down to sign the papers relinquishing his parental rights—not that he'd ever exercised them.

My heart pounded as I took the phone. His voice was unfamiliar, yet there was something gentle in his tone. He said he wanted to make sure this was what I wanted—that I was happy and safe—before he signed the papers. I told him I was. My world was with Mom and Dad, with the family I knew and loved. He listened, and then he let go.

The process wasn't simple. We had to go through a home study. I had my own attorney representing me, ensuring that this was truly in my best interest. And then the day came—the day we went to court.

I'll never forget walking into that courtroom. I was 11 years old—awkward, overwhelmed, and fully convinced the judge could read minds. The air was heavy with the seriousness of the moment, and my chest felt tight with a mix of excitement and fear. The judge sat high up on his chair, larger than life and so imposing. His black robe added to his authority, making him seem even taller and broader than he was.

My legs felt like Jell-O as I stood there, terrified that he might say no, that my adoption wouldn't be approved. That I wouldn't get to be a Hucke like the rest of my family. That I would have to stay a Slusser. The sharp crack of the gavel startled me, the sound bouncing off the walls and echoing in my ears. My heart jumped, its pounding almost drowning out everything else.

The judge's deep baritone voice followed, filling the room. It was steady and commanding, but also, kind—like a big, rumbling bear who you knew could be gentle if he wanted to be.

When he spoke to me, it wasn't scary—it was almost comforting.

He looked down at me and smiled, his face softening in a way that made him seem less imposing. He asked me a few questions, his voice kind and reassuring, each word steady and deliberate. At one point, he even made a joke, asking if I wanted to change any other part of my name while we were at it. For a moment, the tension in the room lifted, and a small chuckle rippled through the adults behind me. But I was too scared to laugh or speak, so I just shook my head no, my hands clasped tightly in front of me to stop them from trembling. Everyone was looking at me now, waiting for my answer to the most important question of all.

The judge leaned forward slightly, his eyes meeting mine as he asked, *"Do you want Charles Hucke to adopt you and be your dad forever?"*

My throat felt dry, and I could barely breathe. The weight of the moment pressed down on me. I glanced at Mom, her warm smile giving me courage, and then at Chuck. He looked back at me with hope in his eyes, an unspoken promise shining there. I took a shaky breath, the words barely audible as I answered, *"Yes."*

The judge smiled broadly, nodding as if I had made the best decision in the world. With another sharp crack of the gavel, he signed the adoption decree and said the words I had been longing to hear, *"Your name is now Melissa Jean Hucke."* In that moment, a wave of relief and joy washed over me. My shoulders relaxed, and my legs no longer felt like they might give out. Finally, I belonged.

I was part of the family in every sense of the word. Dad had chosen me, just as God chooses each of us. As we left the courtroom, I held my head a little higher, a new name and a new sense of belonging tucked safely in my heart.

The day Dad adopted me was more than just a legal formality—it was a reflection of God's love.

Just as Dad chose me, God chooses each of us, welcoming us into His family with open arms and an unshakable promise of belonging.

When I was in my early teens, I desperately wanted to meet my birth father, Allen, and know what he was like …

What he looked like …

If he loved me.

I was his daughter. At 14 years old, I begged my mom to help me find him. I had this deep, aching need to know him. He was in my thoughts constantly in one way or another. You could say I was obsessed, and you would be correct. I'd pass men around his age and wonder … *"Is that Allen?"* I didn't know what he looked like except for a few pictures from when I was an infant.

I would daydream all these lovely scenarios—what he did for a living, how he would show up one day out of the blue, tell me how much he loved me, how he had wanted to be a part of my life all along but couldn't. Grandiose stories about what had kept him away until now. I had a wonderfully active imagination. Too bad I didn't write those stories down. They could have made some interesting tales.

Mom couldn't understand why it was so important to me to find him and know him. She couldn't understand the hole I wanted—*no*, needed—to fill. An ache I couldn't explain. A gap that followed me everywhere. A love-shaped wound I never asked for. Mom grew up with her parents and her siblings. They were always there—through the good and the bad.

Me?

I had questions. *Burning* questions.

And she was *angry* that I wanted to look for this man who left and never looked back. A man who never fought for me ... who never even asked to see me. She couldn't understand why I wanted any contact with him. To her, it seemed baffling—maybe even insulting. *Why* would I want anything to do with him when I had Dad around? Dad—the man who, from the day he met me, treated me like a princess, treated me as his *adored* daughter.

Dad was here. Present. Always eager to do anything for me. *Why wasn't that enough?* Why did I need anything more?

She didn't understand, and at 14, I didn't have the words—or the maturity—to explain the need I had for Allen in my life. How could I explain the *ache* I felt, the space only *he* could fill, when I didn't fully understand it myself?

The arguments weren't explosive or loud, but they were *heavy*. I could feel her disappointment in every sigh, every furrowed brow, and the way her voice tightened whenever Allen's name came up. She never outright forbade me from looking, but her resistance was clear. *"Why?"* she would ask, exasperated. *"Why do you care? He hasn't cared about you—not once. Not when you were sick. Not when you had birthdays. Not ever. Why do you want to find him now?"*

Each time she asked, I felt like I had no good answer. No defense that wouldn't hurt her even more. Her words hung in the air, a reminder of all the times Allen *hadn't* been there. All the reasons I *should* have let go of the idea of him entirely.

But I couldn't.

Even at 14, I knew there was something incomplete in me. A part of my identity that felt like a blank page, waiting to be filled.

I needed answers. I needed to *understand*.

Yet, I gave up my search.

Not because I wanted to.

But because I didn't want to upset my mom.

I didn't want her to be mad at me or to feel like I was choosing Allen over her and Dad.

Truthfully, I *hated* the tension. I hated the way she would look at me with hurt in her eyes. Or the way her voice would turn sharp, laced with disappointment and anger, if I brought it up. And I *hated* how she could make me feel guilty with just a few carefully chosen words.

Mom was good at that—making me second-guess myself, making me feel like I was selfish for wanting something she couldn't understand.

So, I *stopped* looking. I tucked away my questions, buried my curiosity, and tried to ignore the hollow feeling it left behind.

But it wasn't easy.

It *hurt*, even at 14, in ways I didn't have the tools to process. The longing didn't disappear—it just went quiet, sitting *heavily* in the background of my life. I told myself it was better this way. Better to keep the peace. Better not to push it.

But deep down, I *knew* the ache wouldn't go away until I found the answers I was searching for.

Mom was upset.

But Dad? Dad was *understanding*. He hurt *for* me. He knew I didn't love him any less. He didn't want me hurt by Allen, but he knew I *needed* to know. So, when Mom was telling me *"No,"* Dad was telling me, *"It's okay, I understand, and I'll help you with whatever you want to do."*

After crying and praying—and asking God to help me know what to do, to tell me what was best—I came to a decision. At 14 years old, I still had some growing up and maturing to do. It would be best to wait until I was 18. Until I was *an adult.*

Looking back, I find it funny. I actually *thought* four years would make me an adult, capable of handling anything I would learn or go through. On one hand, it's rather *impressive* that I was mature enough at 14 to *realize* I needed to grow up some more. But on the other hand, it's rather *funny* that I thought it would *only* take four years, and I'd be there.

But that's what I thought.

So, I waited.

While I waited, life went on.

I was in high school, trying to juggle teenage drama with the deeper, heavier questions I carried.

One of the courses I took was creative writing. I *loved* it—it gave me a chance to channel some of my thoughts and feelings. Of course, Allen became a chosen subject more than once. Those early, hurting pieces of poetry were raw and full of questions. They weren't exactly literary masterpieces, but they were *honest.*

I kept those poems, tucked away like little time capsules of my teenage heartache.

Looking back now, they feel like glimpses into a younger version of myself—one that was trying to make sense of the pain, to find answers through words. Writing was my way of reaching out into the void, hoping someone—or maybe just my future self—might understand.

I started praying.

How was I *ever* going to find this man? Remember, this was *before* the internet and social media. I knew his name. *William Allen Slusser.* I knew he was from Heavener, Oklahoma. I knew he was an only child. I knew his mother was murdered four years before I was born.

Not a lot to go on, don't you agree?

But I have friends. Amazing friends. Quite a few in law enforcement. Do you see where I'm going here? Yes, one of them took the little bit of information I had—and *found him.*

It didn't take him long.

Hope is an interesting thing. We hope for many things over our lifetimes. Some are small, silly things, while others are huge and life-changing. I spent so much of my life hoping for a dad—whether it was to have one at all or to meet my birth father and learn about him and his family. There was always the hope that he was out there and that I would meet him.

God gave me a wonderful dad. He wasn't perfect, but he was perfect for me. He loved me, was there for me no matter what was going on. He supported me in all my decisions. He was there if it went beautifully, and things were roses and sunshine. He was there if everything went south, and I crashed and burned. He was there to pick up the pieces of my broken heart and shattered dreams.

I had hope that I would meet my birth father, and he would do that too. That he would love me and want to be a part of my life. Allen was out there somewhere. When I found him only to have him pull his disappearing act again, I was angry and heartbroken. What was wrong with me that he didn't want to be a part of my life?

It took me a long time—days, months, years, even decades—to realize it wasn't me. It was never me. It was Allen. It was his feelings, his character, his history that was the catalyst for whether he was in my life or not. It was his choices in life that bled over and impacted my life and how I perceived what was happening.

While Allen's absence created questions I carried for years, Dad's love and actions gave me answers in a way I never expected. He was the kind of father who didn't just step into the role—he redefined it.

From the moment Dad walked into my life, he was there. He wasn't just present—he was intentional. He made sure I knew I mattered, that I was part of every decision, every step forward. From day one, I wasn't just a kid who came with the package; I **was** the package.

When he and Mom decided to move in together, it wasn't as simple as packing boxes and signing a lease. Mom told me that if I didn't want to go, she was going to leave me with Granny and Granddaddy. But Chuck wouldn't hear of it. He looked at her and said, **"No. If she's not going, then you're not going."** We were a package deal, and he made sure I knew that. It wasn't just words—it was action. He made me feel wanted, like I was more than just part of the equation. I was the whole thing.

When he proposed to Mom, he didn't just ask her. He asked me, too. I was only eight years old, but that didn't matter. He knelt down, looked me in the eye, and asked if I was okay with him marrying my mom. He told me that if I wasn't on board, it wasn't going to happen. Even then, at such a young age, I felt the weight of what that meant. He wasn't just marrying her—he was choosing me, too.

He never stopped choosing me. From the big milestones to the smallest moments, Dad was always there. He showed up for every important event in my life—school plays, dance recitals, first days of school. He didn't just show up; he showed me I was important to him.

He even made time for the little moments, the ones that didn't seem like much to the world but meant everything to me.

When I started driving, he taught me how to make minor repairs on my car. Not just the basics, like changing the oil or a tire—though I learned those, too—but the kind of things that would keep me safe and get me home if something went wrong. He wanted me to feel capable and independent. It wasn't just about the car; it was about making sure I knew he had my back, even when he wasn't there.

And then, there was my 16th birthday. That day, as I sat in class, a delivery arrived of 16 long-stem roses. They weren't from some high school boyfriend or a secret admirer. They were from Dad.

He wanted to be the first man to give me flowers. He wanted to set the bar, to make sure I knew I was worth thoughtful gestures and grand displays of love. He told me later, "I wanted to make sure the first guy to give you flowers was your dad. So, you'd always know you deserved them."

If Brad Paisley's song "He Didn't Have to Be" had been around when I got married, it would've been my pick for our father-daughter dance. It's like that song was written straight out of my story—the man who didn't have to show up but did. And in doing so, he changed everything.

Then there was Allen. Allen, who was never there. No roses, no life lessons, no shared moments. For most of my childhood, he was a shadow—a question mark in the shape of a man. He didn't call, didn't write, didn't show up. He wasn't there when I needed someone to teach me how to ride a bike or when I got my first report card. He wasn't there to see me grow up, to know who I was, or to show me who he was.

Allen was an absence I didn't understand, a hole I didn't know how to fill. But Dad? Dad filled that space with love, laughter, and a steady presence that never wavered. Where Allen left silence, Dad gave me stories. Where Allen gave me questions, Dad gave me answers. And where Allen gave me emptiness, Dad gave me belonging. Even as Dad's love surrounded me, the questions about Allen lingered.

Little did I know, the answers would come—but not without challenges, and certainly not in the way I expected.

Field Notes:
Evidence for Healing

Love is more about presence than perfection, and earthly glimpses of love point us to God's perfect love.

REFLECTION QUESTIONS

- Who in your life has loved you by choice, not obligation?
- What does "being chosen" mean to you now, as an adult?
- Are there people you've struggled to receive love from?

ENCOURAGEMENT

God often sends people to love us in the very ways we need most. Don't miss that miracle just because it doesn't look like the version you imagined.

WRITING PROMPT

Write about someone who stepped into your life and showed up consistently. How did their love rewrite part of your story?

SCRIPTURE ANCHOR

"See what great love the Father has lavished on us, that we should be called children of God! And that is what we are! The reason the world does not know us is that it did not know him."   **— 1 John 3:1**

PRAYER

Thank You, Lord, for the ones who stayed when others walked away. Help me learn to trust again. Make me someone who stays—who loves not because they must, but because they choose to.

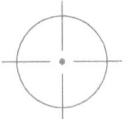

CASE FILE #004

The Search Begins

*"And hope does not put us to shame, because God's love has
been poured out into our hearts through the Holy Spirit,
who has been given to us."*
– Romans 5:5

L
ife is full of twists and turns, isn't it? My search for my roots
brought plenty of both: the kind of losses that cut deep
and blessings that snuck up on me, reminding me just how
beautiful a family can be. I thought I was on a quest just to find my
father, to fill that missing piece of where I belonged. But along the
way, I realized God had been weaving His own story, one I hadn't
seen until now.

For every loss, there's usually something gained, even if it
doesn't feel that way at first. There are always two sides to the story,
whether it's joy or heartache. What really matters is how we face
those moments and what we choose to do with them.

My life has been more of a rollercoaster than a merry-go-round, that's for sure. Funny thing is that I'm not even a fan of rollercoasters! But the analogy? That's a whole different story. I honestly believe that without the lows, we can't fully appreciate the highs.

Think about it. If life just moseyed along with perfect weather every day, no clouds, birds singing nonstop, at first, it'd be amazing. You'd step outside, take a deep breath, and let it fill your soul.

But after a while? You'd stop noticing. You'd start to miss the rain, the sounds, the smells, the way it makes everything feel so fresh and clean. Rain fills lakes, streams, and ponds, making things new again. And don't forget the rainbow: our reminder of God's promises shining after the storm.

Growing up, I desperately wanted a dad—someone to call Daddy, someone to carry me on his shoulders, teach me about life, and protect me as I grew. I didn't think I had that, and I longed for it with all my heart. What I didn't understand back then—and what you've probably seen by now—is that God didn't give me just one. He sent a handful of men, each filling part of that role in their own way.

But it started with just one—Granddaddy. He was my mom's dad, and he doted on me like no one else. When he got home from work, he'd settle into his orange recliner in the living room with a western or a WWII show on the TV, and I'd curl up in his lap like it was my own little throne. He'd take me fishing with my uncles and aunt, or Granny, and he would whisk me away on road trips to visit family—or even to Disney World.

When Granddaddy passed unexpectedly at just 58 years old, it felt like the world shifted beneath me. His death left a gap I didn't know how to fill. The warmth of his lap, the thrill of fishing trips, he'd been my anchor, my steady place. Losing him only deepened the ache I already felt, that longing for a father's love and security.

I still hold onto memories, like the winter we visited Granny's family in Missouri. Somewhere along the way, it snowed. For a little girl from Texas who had never seen snow, it was nothing short of magical. Granddaddy made those moments unforgettable, and even now, they bring a bittersweet smile to my face.

Mom had told me that if we saw snow, I should bring some back for her since she had to stay home and work. Being the sweet, loving daughter I was, I grabbed a Mason jar, went outside, and carefully built a tiny snowman to fit inside. Proud of my frosty creation, I sealed him up, and off we went, heading back to Texas.

Unfortunately, my poor little snowman didn't make it home. Rockport, Missouri, to Channelview, Texas, is a long journey— especially when traveling with a small child who has a tiny bladder. Add in all the lovely family members you just *must* stop and visit along the way, and, well … things happen.

We stopped in Vinton, Louisiana, to see Granddaddy's parents, and that's where my snowman met his untimely demise. They had a roaring fire going to keep the chill out of the house, and it was so nice and toasty warm. Naturally, I couldn't leave my snowman alone in the car—he might get scared, and besides, he'd get cold! So, in the house he came. I set him on the hearth next to me while we soaked up the warmth.

After a bit, Great-Grandma Smith took me to the kitchen for a little glass of grape juice. I sat at the bar, happily sipping and playing with one of those Drinking Bird toys. (You know the one—a little bird that dips its beak into a glass of water when you tap its head. They were all the rage in the '70s.)

By the time we were ready to head out for the final stretch home, I went to retrieve my snowman ... only to find a sad little jar of water.

I was devastated. I'd worked so hard to build him, to keep him safe and snug in his jar, only for him to melt before I could give him to Mom. My tiny snowman was gone, and I was crushed.

In that little peek at my childhood, you can see what I mean—the highs and joys of experiencing snow for the first time and building a tiny snowman, paired with the valleys of disappointment when my snowman didn't make it to Mom in Channelview as anything more than a jar of water.

As I grew, moments like these became bittersweet—reminders of the father I longed for, the one I wished had been there to share in both the highs and the lows.

As I've mentioned, one of these high points in my life was Chuck Hucke—my dad. He wasn't the man who gave me life, but he was the man God sent to us and who chose to be there for me.

Dad never tried to stop me from searching for my birth father. He didn't take it personally. Instead, he stood by me every step of the way, helping however he could. He understood the ache I felt— that sense of missing a piece of myself. And even as I searched for answers elsewhere, he encouraged me to find what I needed, always reminding me that his love was steady and unwavering.

In his quiet, steadfast way, he taught me that being a parent isn't about biology—it's about choice, showing up, and love.

Looking back, I realize how blessed I was that God brought him into my life. But unfortunately for most of my life, I didn't see it—not really.

I was a typical self-absorbed teen, too caught up in my own world to recognize how incredible he was. Sure, there were moments when I'd get glimpses of how lucky I was, but it didn't truly hit me until I learned the full truth about Allen and Danny. That's when it all came together, and I saw the gift I'd been given in Chuck—my dad.

I felt like my identity was tied to who my father was. At least, that's how it felt as a teenager. I desperately wanted to know where I came from—who my family was. I wanted the stories. The kind of stories I grew up hearing about Mom's side of the family: the sweet, the funny, the downright quirky.

How much do you know about your own family tree? The good, the bad, the awkward, and yes, even the ugly? Let's face it, we all have skeletons rattling around in our closets—it's just a matter of if (and when) they decide to see the light of day. And once they do, well, there's no putting them back.

Growing up, one of the few things I knew about Allen and his family was that he was part Cherokee, as well as the only child of his parents: Jay and Dorothy Clark Slusser. They divorced when he was young, and Allen's mother, Dorothy, had a tragic story.

Dorothy worked as a nurse but struggled with substance abuse. You may remember that back in 1964—four years before I was born—Allen's mother met a man in a bar, took him home, and never made it out alive. That loss would cast a long shadow over his life. The man stabbed her to death, confessed when questioned, and went to prison for her murder. Since she was gone long before I came along, I never met her, and the only glimpses I had of her life came through scattered details—most of which were difficult to hear.

Allen himself had a rough childhood for many reasons, but he had one bright light—his grandmother, Lola. She was the sweetest little lady, a woman of deep faith who read her Bible daily. When I finally found Allen and met his family, only two people truly welcomed me with open arms: Lola and her son, Paul. They didn't judge me based on Allen's reputation or the kind of man he was. They simply accepted me for who I was.

Looking back, I realize how God was working quietly in those moments. Even as some family members kept their distance, worried I'd be like Allen, God was filling the gaps. He was showing me that I wasn't alone, that His love and acceptance were greater than anything I could find here on earth.

I didn't realize how special it was at the time—but now I do. Hindsight has a way of rearranging everything, like puzzle pieces falling into place. From this distance, I can see where God was working all along, gently filling in the gaps—even when I couldn't feel it.

Looking back now, I can see how God used every relationship, every disappointment, and every moment of searching to shape me. In those moments of hurt, I didn't realize it, but He was preparing me for something more. And the truth is, my search was only just beginning.

Growing up, I wanted nothing more than to find my father—a man who could answer the questions that kept me awake at night.

But as I set out on this journey, I quickly realized that finding him wouldn't be simple. And the answers I uncovered would be more complicated than I ever imagined.

Starting felt impossible. Where do you even begin to find someone who vanished from your life before you were old enough to remember them? It wasn't like I could just type his name into Google—this was 1987, and the internet wasn't even a blip on our radar yet. My "resources" consisted of a rotary phone, a library card, and maybe, if I were lucky, a helpful operator willing to track down an old phone number.

One of the wonderful men at church was a police officer. He knew how much I wanted to find and meet Allen. He asked me a few questions to get what information I had, and then he did his thing. The next Sunday at church, he handed me a slip of paper with Allen's address and phone number. It was April 1987. I was 18 years old, preparing to graduate from high school.

Can you imagine how excited, as well as nervous, I was, standing there holding that little slip of paper?

Even in my naiveté, I knew that my life was about to change.

How could it not change?

I had valuable information to finally be able to reach out and speak to the man that I owed my existence to.

I called Allen for the first time, my heart pounding as I dialed the California number. The phone rang, and then an answering machine picked up. "Hello, Allen," I said, my voice trembling. "It's Missy, your daughter. I'd really like to talk to you. Please call me back."

I hung up, half-expecting him to call back immediately. But the days stretched on, and my anticipation turned to uncertainty. Every day, I left more messages—short, hopeful, and painfully polite.

By the end of the month, my polite pleas had turned into daily rituals: "It's me again, Allen. I just want to talk."

Still, silence.

Finally, after a month of leaving messages every day, he called me back.

The phone was heavy in my hand, my fingers gripping the receiver just a little too tightly as I pressed it to my ear. My heart pounded, each beat echoing in my chest like a drumroll leading up to the moment I had been waiting for my whole life.

And then—his voice.

It was deeper than I had imagined, familiar yet completely unknown. The moment he said, "Hello?" my breath caught in my throat. For the first time in almost nine years, I was hearing my birth father's voice.

I was sitting on the kitchen floor, my back against the cabinets, knees pulled up as I twisted the long phone cord around my fingers. It stretched from the wall, tangling and looping as if trying to keep up with the whirlwind of emotions swirling inside me. My entire world had shrunk down to this moment, this conversation.

At first, I was nervous—what if I said the wrong thing? What if he didn't like me? But the more we talked, the more the fear melted away. We talked about everything and nothing all at once. His voice was warm, steady, and full of something I desperately craved—connection.

Time disappeared. Minutes blurred into hours. Three of them, in fact.

By the time we finally hung up, I was euphoric. I sat there on the kitchen floor, the silence around me now deafening compared to the lively conversation that had just filled my ears. My face ached from smiling; my heart soared.

I was finally talking to my birth father.

I was giddy.

All my dreams were finally coming true.

I had a father.

Life was grand.

I was finally getting to ask Allen some of the questions I had. Some were hard, and the answers were super important to me, while others were just silly ones that weren't important in the grand scheme of things.

Allen said he loved me.

I needed to hear that.

Allen told me so many things that day. Words I had been longing to hear for as long as I could remember. He said he loved me, that he had always loved me. He said he missed me, that not a day had gone by when he didn't think about me.

And then came the promises.

He promised to stay in my life, to get to know me, to be the father I'd been missing. He swore he would call the next weekend so we could talk again. I was so happy that day. For days afterward, really. I was floating on a cloud, replaying every word of that conversation in my mind,

He had said the words I thought would heal the ache I carried for so long.

"I love you."

"I've missed you."

"I'm so excited to get to know you."

I told everyone. I was giddy with joy.

I HAD TALKED TO ALLEN!! MY FATHER!!

It felt like my life was finally starting to make sense. Like all those years of wondering, of feeling like something was missing, were finally over.

I didn't know it then, of course, but I would eventually discover that at least half or more of what he said to me that day was lies.

As I hung up the phone from that conversation, I was on cloud nine. It was so wonderful to have finally had the chance to speak with him. To hear his voice and know what he sounded like. To hear that he loved me and wished he could have been there while I was growing up.

Then ... crickets. Worse than crickets.

He changed his phone number. He moved. Left no forwarding address. He had been in California. But now? Who knows.

My friend offered to find him again, but I passed on his offer. If Allen was going to pull a vanishing act, then I didn't need him in my life. I was hurt and angry. I still had most of the same questions because even though I had spoken to him that day for three hours, we didn't get my questions covered. He did ask things about me and my childhood. So, he must have been interested in some form or another.

But the happiness that had buoyed me after our call drained away, replaced by a familiar ache.

The pain of abandonment. Again. The heartbreak. The anger.

I tried to tell myself it didn't matter, that I shouldn't have expected anything different. But deep down, it did matter. It mattered so much.

I had let myself believe. Let myself hope. I had allowed myself to imagine a different future—one where he was in my life, where I had a father who wanted to know me, to love me. And now, all I had were broken promises and silence.

It felt like a void, an endless reminder of all the things I would never have, all the things I would never be to him.

I wasn't important enough.

I wasn't worth the effort.

What was it about me that made him leave? Why wasn't I enough for him to stay? Was I so horrible that my own father couldn't bear to stick around? The questions echoed louder than I wanted to admit, each one cutting deeper than the last.

Those thoughts burned through me, turning the hope to which I had once clung into anger. Anger at him for making promises he had no intention of keeping. Anger at myself for believing him. The heartbreak was raw, a wound reopened and left to fester. I had wanted so badly for his words to be true. I had wanted him to be the father I had dreamed of. But dreams, I was learning, didn't always come true.

Anger quickly became my armor. I told myself, forget him. I don't need him. And I made a decision: I wasn't going to waste any more time searching for a man who clearly didn't want to be found. I had better things to do. Like finish high school, figure out what came next, and move forward with my life.

Field Notes:
Evidence for Healing

Searching for truth takes courage—but God is always ready to meet us in the unknown.

REFLECTION QUESTIONS

- Have you ever gone searching for someone or something that felt essential to who you are?

- What emotions did that search stir up—fear, hope, anger, courage?

- How do you process disappointment when someone doesn't show up the way you needed them to?

ENCOURAGEMENT

Searching doesn't make you weak—it makes you brave. It takes courage to chase after truth, even when there's no guarantee of what you'll find. God sees your pursuit. He walks with you through every unanswered call, every dead end, every tear-filled prayer. And He never disappears—He stays.

WRITING PROMPT

Write about a time when you hoped for something or someone ... and were let down. What did that moment teach you about expectations? About trust? About yourself?

SCRIPTURE ANCHOR

"You will seek me and find me when you seek me with all your heart." – **Jeremiah 29:13**

PRAYER

Father God, You know how much I've longed for answers. For connection. For someone to show up and say, "You matter." The silence has been loud, and the waiting has felt endless. I've tried to fill the ache, to make sense of the questions, to understand why I was left behind. But through all of it—You were there. When I called and no one answered, You heard me. When I felt rejected, You reminded me I was chosen. When I searched for a father, You stayed close as the one who never left. God, heal the places in me that still hurt. Quiet the voices that say I'm not enough. Help me to see my worth through Your eyes—not the eyes of someone who walked away. I release the pain of unmet expectations, and I hold onto the truth that I am deeply known and fully loved by You. Thank You for walking with me through the questions. Thank You for being the answer I didn't know I was looking for. In Jesus' name, Amen.

I Wasn't Done Needing Him

"Call to me and I will answer you and tell you great and
unsearchable things you do not know."
– Jeremiah 33:3

Ithrew myself into the whirlwind of growing up. I graduated high school and took a job waiting tables at Pizza Hut, babysitting on the side to make a little extra money. And then, something unexpected happened—something that nudged my life in an entirely new direction. I went on a blind date.

Dating wasn't exactly my strong suit. In fact, I was so shy in high school that I didn't go on my first date until I was 17. I spent most of that time worried about doing the right thing, too nervous to relax or enjoy myself.

But this blind date? It marked the beginning of a chapter I didn't see coming, one that would change everything. I had become friends with a family whose children I took care of for a couple of years. They had someone they wanted to set me up with. They were one of my favorite families to babysit for—I liked the parents and the kids both. That made it easy to say yes when she, the mom, wanted to set me up with a guy who worked with her husband. We made plans for the four of us to go to dinner in Houston.

I graduated from high school on June 6, 1987. Just a week later, I found myself agreeing to a blind date—because, why not? I was young, full of possibility and the idea of meeting someone new felt exciting. I had no idea that one simple *yes* would set off a chain of events that would change everything.

He was charming, attentive, and said all the right things. He made me feel special—wanted. After years of wondering where I truly belonged, the idea of someone choosing *me* was intoxicating. We spent hours talking, dreaming, and planning, caught up in a romance that felt like something out of a fairytale. Before I knew it, we were inseparable.

And then, not long after we met, he proposed.

To everyone's surprise—including maybe my own—I said yes. The words left my mouth before my brain had time to fully process them. It was thrilling, the kind of head-spinning romance that movies were made of. One minute, I was a high school graduate figuring out my next steps, and the next, I was a fiancée planning a wedding.

We set the date for August 29, 1987. Just weeks away.

It was a whirlwind courtship, the kind that sweeps you up so fast you don't have time to ask yourself if your feet are still on the ground. Every day was filled with anticipation, with plans, with excitement. But beneath the exhilaration, there were moments of doubt—small, quiet whispers in the back of my mind. *Is this too fast? Am I ready for this? Do I really know him?*

But love—or what I thought was love—was louder.

And so, I ignored the whispers and held onto the dream. Because for the first time in my life, I felt like I had a future that was mine to create.

Unfortunately, it would be my first real taste of romantic heartbreak—the kind that knocks the wind out of you and leaves a scar when love doesn't turn out the way you hoped.

I was having doubts—real, nagging, deep-in-my-gut doubts. But I was too much of a wimp to call it off myself. So instead, I did what I thought was the next best thing—I prayed.

> *"God, if this is a mistake, if I'm not supposed to marry him ... please, just take care of it for me."*

And He did.

But what I didn't anticipate—what I wasn't prepared for—was how much it would still hurt.

I had asked God to step in, and He had answered my prayer in no uncertain terms. My fiancée sat me down, looked me in the eye, and told me he didn't want to marry me after all. He didn't love me. That was bad enough. But then came the real gut punch.

He was going back to the girl he had been engaged to before we met.

Just like that, it was over.

I felt like I'd been gutted. The air was sucked out of the room. My stomach twisted, my heart clenched, and for a moment, I thought I might actually collapse under the weight of it.

He didn't want me.

Again, I wasn't good enough—at least, that's what it felt like. I wasn't wanted. I wasn't loved. And in that moment, I wondered if I ever really had been. Had I just been fooling myself? Had I seen something that was never actually there? The questions swirled, each one cutting a little deeper. Maybe I wasn't enough. Maybe I had never been enough.

Either way, I was left standing there, alone, with nothing but the echo of his rejection and the unbearable weight of my own unworthiness.

I had prayed for this. I had literally asked God to take care of it. And He had. But somehow, knowing it was the right thing didn't make it hurt any less. Because rejection—no matter how much you see it coming, no matter how much you try to brace for it—still knocks the wind out of you.

As I sit here writing this, it hits me—like one of those "well, duh" revelations that only land when your heart finally catches up to what your head already knew. That relationship? The one that led to my first engagement? It was born out of rebound. Plain and simple. I was still reeling from Allen's disappearing act—still carrying the sting of that three-hour phone call followed by radio silence. I didn't have the tools to process that kind of abandonment, not back then. So, when someone else came along and said they loved me, I clung to it like a life raft. It wasn't love. It wasn't right. But it felt like being chosen. And I was desperate for that.

Eventually, I decided I needed to get out of town—away from the sympathetic looks, the awkward conversations, and the people who, bless their hearts, didn't quite know what to say to me. Everywhere I went, I felt like I was wearing a giant sign that read: *Heartbroken. Engaged, then dumped. Proceed with caution.*

Looking back, I doubt people thought about me nearly as much as I imagined they did. But at the time, it felt like my failed engagement was the talk of the town. Maybe it was. Or maybe I was just too caught up in my own feelings to see past them. Either way, I knew one thing—I needed a fresh start. It was time to get out of town!

I'd always loved kids, and they'd always loved me right back. Babysitting had been second nature to me for as long as I could remember. I could calm a fussy toddler, wrangle a group of rowdy kids, and get even the most stubborn little one to sleep. So, I did what I knew best—I leaned into what came naturally.

I found a nanny agency, applied, and before I knew it, I had a job lined up in the Washington, D.C. area—specifically, Potomac, Maryland.

And just like that, I packed my bags and left.

I went from the familiar warmth of my small Texas hometown to a place that felt entirely different. Suddenly, I was living in a house with a family I had never met before, caring for three energetic boys who kept me on my toes from the moment I walked in the door. I quickly learned that little boys don't just play—they wrestle, they climb, they run full speed at all times. They were loud, messy, and absolutely wonderful.

That year stretched me. It was my first time truly being on my own, away from my family, my friends, and everything comfortable.

There were nights I felt lonely, nights when the ache of homesickness hit hard. But there were also days filled with laughter, sweet moments when the youngest would reach for my hand, or when one of the older boys would proudly show me a Lego creation as if he had just built the Taj Mahal.

I grew up that year.

At the end of my contract, I returned home, feeling different in ways I couldn't quite explain. I had left as a heartbroken girl trying to outrun her past, and I came back a little stronger, a little wiser, and with a newfound sense of independence.

But it turns out, I wasn't done yet.

A year or so later, I packed up again and headed back to Maryland for another stint as their nanny. That time, I only stayed for six months before returning to Texas for good.

And as much as I love Texas, I have to admit—fall in Maryland was breathtaking. I had never seen colors like that in my life. The trees looked like they had been painted with every shade of red, orange, and gold imaginable. And the snow! Growing up where I did, snow was something you wished for but rarely got. That first snowfall felt magical, like stepping into a snow globe.

Do I miss the fall colors? Absolutely!

The snow? Not so much. Give me Texas sunsets and warm weather any day.

Maybe that's the thing about life—you think you know what you want, what you prefer, where you belong. And then, something shifts. A thought, a question, a feeling that refuses to be ignored.

For me, that question had been simmering for years. I kept brushing it aside, telling myself it didn't matter, that I'd get to it *someday*.

But *someday* wasn't coming fast enough. And I needed answers.

Allen was out there somewhere. He existed. And in my heart, I believed that if I could just find him, everything would fall into place. And then—I did. When I was 18, we spoke on the phone. It was brief, but it felt like the start of something. Maybe even everything. But just as quickly as he appeared, he was gone again.

No explanation. No follow-up. Just silence.

I replayed every word of that conversation, searching for something—some clue, some reason—why he left. What was wrong with me that he didn't want to be a part of my life? That he could walk away so easily?

Over and over, the questions circled, each one carving out a little more of my self-worth.

But the truth? Nothing was wrong with me. Absolutely nothing. It took me years—days, months, *decades*—to fully understand that. To let it settle deep in my bones, past the hurt and the doubt.

It wasn't me.

It was never me.

It was Allen. His feeling, his character, his history—those were the forces that determined whether he was in my life or not. It was his choices, not my worth.

But his choices bled over into my life, and for so long, I let them shape the way I saw myself. I let them define me, make me question my value, make me wonder if I was unlovable, unwanted.

The weight of someone else's brokenness had settled onto my shoulders, and I carried it far too long.

But not anymore.

You might remember—I've mentioned the time I talked to Allen when I was ten. Let's just say it wasn't exactly a heartwarming Hallmark moment. I was a nervous wreck, he was basically a stranger, and I definitely wasn't about to start unloading my childhood emotions on the man who'd been MIA since day one. Just because he helped kick off my existence didn't mean I was ready to roll out the red carpet.

Still—awkward silence or not—that call did what it needed to do.

I moved along with my life. I fell in love for the first time. I got engaged. I had my heart broken. I moved across the United States from Texas to the East Coast. And then back home to Texas. Twice!

Still, a part of me was that little girl with all those bloody questions! By the time I had reached 21 years of age, I had decided: Enough is enough. I am going to find Allen, meet him, and get my answers once and for all!

At this time, I was working as a nanny for an attorney that I had known for years. I babysat for them when I was in high school. Coach, the attorney's father, was a private investigator. Guess who helped me this go-around? Yep. Coach.

I gave him what information I had: where Allen had lived when I was 18 and anything else I could think of. A couple of hours later, he called me. Coach had spoken to one of Allen's cousins and confirmed where Allen was living and working.

Great!

Did I call?

Nope. Are you crazy? I had learned my lesson the hard way the first time around. I spoke with my bosses—they were wonderful, kind, and understanding. Both of their children are adopted, so they could understand to a degree what I was going through. I took a couple of days off work, then with Mom and my younger sister Christina, I drove from Cut-n-Shoot, Texas to Heavener, Oklahoma. By this point, Mom had decided she wasn't going to let me face Allen alone—she couldn't protect me from the past, but she could be there with me now, and that was her way of showing up.

We checked into a hotel down the street from Lola's house. Then Mom called her.

She told Lola who she was, that she had me there, and that I wanted to meet her. (Remember, Lola was Allen's grandmother, and she was in her 80s at that time.) They set a time for us to go over to her house later that day.

When we arrived, Lola opened the door, giving me the biggest smile and hug. Lola's embrace was warm and unhurried, like she'd been waiting for me her whole life. Her kitchen smelled of coffee and something sweet, and her soft voice made me feel, for the first time, like I truly belonged. She was so happy to finally meet me.

After a brief visit, Mom told Lola that I really wanted to meet Allen. We loaded up into the car and drove to Poteau, the next town over. Allen worked at the Western Auto there. Remember the last time I had called him, and he pulled a disappearing act? I learned from my mistake. No call was made to warn Allen of my impending arrival.

When we pulled into the parking lot of Western Auto, my heart pounded so loudly I was certain everyone in the car could hear it. I pressed my hands against my lap, trying to still their slight tremble, but nothing could quiet the storm inside me.

As we parked, I stole a glance at the others. Their faces held a mix of encouragement and concern, silent reminders that I wasn't alone—but this part of the journey was mine to walk. No one could do it for me. They stayed back while I reached for the door handle, my fingers tightening around the cool metal as if bracing for impact.

Stepping out of the car, my legs felt unsteady, like they had suddenly forgotten how to hold me up. The pavement beneath my feet felt more like shifting sand as I made my way toward the entrance. Each step felt heavier than the last, burdened with the weight of anticipation, years of unanswered questions pressing down on me.

I wasn't that wide-eyed 18-year-old anymore, the girl who once longed for a fairytale reunion. Life had hardened some of my edges, made me more cautious, more guarded. This time, I wasn't here for dreams—I was here for something real. Answers. Closure. Maybe even a sense of peace.

The door jingled as I stepped inside, the scent of rubber tires and motor oil filling my lungs. The fluorescent lights buzzed overhead, casting a harsh glow over shelves stocked with wrenches, spark plugs, and cans of oil. I swallowed against the lump rising in my throat.

At the counter, I spotted an older man in a store uniform. My voice felt foreign in my own ears as I asked, "Is Allen here?"

He nodded, not asking any questions, and disappeared into the back.

And just like that, I was alone.

I wandered the aisles, my fingertips ghosting over the rough edges of toolboxes and dusty shelves. My eyes skimmed over the endless rows of automotive supplies, but I wasn't seeing any of it. My heart raced. My stomach twisted into knots. A slow, prickling heat spread from my chest to my face, the kind that came with the collision of nerves and expectation.

Any moment now he would walk out.

And I had no idea what would happen next.

Out of the corner of my eye, I noticed movement, A man was walking toward me, his steps purposeful yet unhurried. I turned to face him, and the moment our eyes met, time seemed to slow. My breath caught in my throat as he introduced himself, his voice calm but slightly curious, as if he wasn't entirely sure who I was yet. "Can I help you with something?" he asked, his tone polite, almost businesslike.

And there he was.

The man I had built up in my mind for years. The man I had imagined countless times, hoping he'd be everything I'd ever wanted in a father.

In that instant, my emotions collided in a chaotic swirl: my heart raced, my hands trembled, I wasn't sure if I wanted to cry, yell, or hug him. Maybe throw up.

My head spun as I stood there, face to face with the man who had been little more than a voice on the phone and a collection of unanswered questions in my mind.

But as I stared at him, searching his face for something—anything—that felt familiar, I realized something else.

No matter what happened in this moment, nothing could undo the years of silence, the void left by his absence. The gap was too wide, the time too long.

Before I could find the words to respond, the bell at the front of the store jingled. Allen glanced over his shoulder, his eyes widening slightly as he spotted his grandmother and my mom entering the store.

The faintest flicker of recognition crossed his face as he turned back to me. "Missy?" he asked, his voice quieter now, tinged with something I couldn't quite place—was it surprise? Curiosity? Guilt? I nodded, my voice caught somewhere between my heart and my throat. "Yes," I managed to say. "It's me."

Over that weekend, I met quite a few people—Lola, Allen, Allen's wife, Lola's son Paul and his wife, as well as a few cousins. Without a doubt, Lola and Paul were the absolute best part.

As for the rest of the family, I can't say I blame them for being cautious about meeting me—about welcoming me in. Given Allen's history, I imagine they had their doubts, maybe even fears. Maybe they wondered if I was anything like him. I wasn't—but I never got the chance to show them that. They never let me close enough to find out for themselves.

Looking back at the days I met Lola and the rest of the family, there's now a cushion—a sort of buffer—that softens the sharp edges of the hurt and angst I felt back then. I wanted so desperately to be loved and accepted, to find a place where I truly belonged. But when you're living in the thick of something, it's hard to see the full picture.

You're trapped in your own little bubble of pain and self-focus, unable to recognize that God is right there with you, holding you, loving you, and waiting for you to notice.

Field Notes:
Evidence for Healing

Persistence in seeking truth reveals more than answers; it reveals God's hand guiding each step.

REFLECTION QUESTIONS

- Have you ever found yourself attaching quickly to someone simply because they showed you attention or affection?

- How did unmet expectations shape your understanding of love or worth?

- What emotions did you carry after meeting someone you'd longed to know—did they match the ones you imagined?

- When has God used disappointment to protect or redirect you?

WRITING PROMPT

Write about a time you hoped someone would show up for you— and they didn't. What did you feel? What did you need in that moment? Now, imagine writing a letter to your younger self at that time. What truth would you want her to know?

ENCOURAGEMENT

Not everyone who reenters your life is meant to stay. Sometimes God allows reconnections to give you clarity, not closeness. You are not defined by the ones who left, the ones who couldn't love you well, or the ones who loved you conditionally. You are deeply known and fiercely loved by the One who never disappears when the conversation gets hard. You don't have to earn that love. It's already yours.

SCRIPTURE ANCHOR

"Ask and it will be given to you; seek and you will find; knock and the door will be opened to you."

— **Matthew 7:7**

PRAYER

Father, I bring You the ache of disappointment—the hurt of being let down by someone I longed to know. Thank You for walking with me through broken expectations and unanswered questions. Help me release the weight of "what could have been" and anchor myself in the truth of who I am in You. Teach me to love without fear, to hope without idolizing people, and to trust You above all. Amen.

I Came to Nanny, Stayed for the Daddy, and Ended Up Queen of the Carpool

"Unless the Lord builds the house, its builders labor in vain."
– Psalm 127:1a

Next stop: 1993. No roadmap, no expectations—just one nanny job, a toddler, and the guy who'd end up being my forever. I was back from the East Coast after my nanny stint, trying to reestablish my life. I had the childcare experience, the references, and let's be honest—I had the Mary Poppins energy. What I didn't have was a plan.

Enter Chuck Rod. (And yes, you read that right—Chuck. Just like my dad. No, it's not a typo. No, it's not a plot twist. Yes, it made for some *very* confusing early conversations. Still does, in fact. And no, I didn't plan it that way. God's got jokes.)

Let me be clear: when I accepted a nanny job in the early '90s, I was just there for the baby snuggles, the steady paycheck, and a little quiet time to read a book while the toddler napped. What I did *not* expect was to meet Chuck Rod: a recently divorced, full-custody dad trying to figure out how to raise his 13-month-old son, Charlie, with nothing but good intentions and a box of diapers. He had no clue how to raise a baby. Not a *single* clue. He was a working man, a provider, and honestly, he was doing his best—but the baby phase was not his strong suit. The bottle-warming days were mostly behind him, but diapering, feeding, and bedtime routines? Let's just say ... bless his heart. I was hired to care for his son but somehow ended up falling for the guy who came with the diaper bag. One minute, I was wiping noses, and the next? I was saying "I do," merging lives, and running the mom-taxi with a minivan full of snacks and sass. Welcome to the chapter where things get *really* interesting.

You know how people say, "God works in mysterious ways?" Well, I say *God has a sense of humor.* One minute you're trying to outrun heartbreak, and the next, you're falling for a guy who doesn't know the difference between formula and milk and thinks a diaper rash just "needs to air out."

He hired me as the nanny. That's it. That's all it was supposed to be.

But from the very first day, I saw something different in Chuck. Here was a man who had every reason to walk away from the hard stuff, and yet he was *in it.* Messy, overwhelmed, winging it—but in it.

At first, I told myself it was just a job—I was the nanny, he was the boss, and I was absolutely not getting attached. But something about that little duo got under my skin. Maybe it was the way Charlie watched his dad like he hung the moon, or how Chuck was clearly making it up as he went—but doing it with full confidence, like every dad manual had his name on the cover. Whatever it was, this didn't feel like your typical nanny gig. There was heart here—and possibly a future plot twist.

I saw the way he looked at his son. The way he tried. The way he showed up, even when he didn't know what he was doing. He didn't run from the challenge. He stood in the gap.

I admired that. And I started falling. First for the baby—because who wouldn't fall for a chubby-cheeked toddler with a giggle like sunshine? And then for the man who was trying so hard to be everything that baby needed.

It started slow. Respect. Laughter. Meals together. Shared routines. And then came the late-night talks, the honest confessions, and the quiet moments when I realized I wasn't just taking care of a baby anymore—I was building a life.

Chuck didn't just fall for me, either. He invited me into his world. And Charlie? He didn't even have to try. That boy owned my heart from the jump.

What started as a temporary job turned into a forever family.

We got married. I became not just the nanny but a mommy. Not just a visitor—but a wife. A partner. A mama bear with a Suburban and a calendar full of doctor's appointments, playdates, and preschool snacks.

We built something out of the mess.

Out of two broken pasts came one beautiful present.

And I'll say this: I never would've guessed that a job posting, and a sweet baby boy, would lead me to the man who would become my safe place.

But God knew.

Once upon a time, I answered a help-wanted ad.

Turns out, God was writing a love story.

What started as a quirky little trio—one dad, one baby, one nanny—blossomed into something wild and wonderful. Over the years, our family of three morphed into parents of four sons and two daughters. We've added two amazing daughters-in-love, four precious grandsons (so far!), and a whole lot of joy, chaos, and grace in between. And who knows? We might not be finished growing yet.

Now I've been a nanny, a mommy, a bonus mom, an adoptive mom, and the newest addition to my resume: Honey (depending on who's yelling across the house).

But let's call it what it is: I'm the Matriarch of Mayhem, and the CEO of "Did You Seriously Just Lick That?" Tiaras off to anyone who dares challenge that title.

Our dinner table's louder, our schedule's packed, and the laundry's never-ending—but my heart? It's never been fuller. I may not have come from a perfect family, but by the grace of God, I helped build one that's perfectly mine.

Out of two broken pasts, we built something beautiful. No, it's not perfect—but by the grace of God, it's ours. It's home. It's perfectly mine.

And yet ... Allen was never far from my mind.

Over the next ten years, I spent time getting to know him—my birth father. I learned some things. Some good, some hard. And one thing I learned with absolute clarity: I had a *fabulous* dad who raised me. I won the jackpot the day Mom prayed—half in doubt, all in desperation—to a God she wasn't even sure existed, asking for someone who would love me as much as he loved her.

God delivered.

Isn't it wild how God answers prayers even when we don't yet belong to Him? The Bible tells us He wants the best for us—and He truly does. He watches over us, loves us, even when we're oblivious to His work or caught up in our own mess.

And then came April 1999.

I was 31 when the phone rang. A distant cousin on the other end. There had been a fire—and Allen was gone.

At first, I assumed the worst. I figured alcohol or carelessness had caused it. Maybe he passed out smoking, maybe it was something else. I was wrong.

The fire department said it was electrical. He died of smoke inhalation. I was stunned. Sad that he was gone. Sad that we didn't have more time. Sad that he'd never get to be a grandfather to my children—to hear their laughter, to see their eyes, to notice the little pieces of him that might have lived on in them.

At his funeral, I said goodbye.

Not just to the man himself, but to everything I had ever hoped he could be.

I said goodbye to the possibility of a relationship, to the conversations we never had, to the memories that would never be made.

I said goodbye to the man who had shaped me in ways I never expected—not through his presence, but through his absence.

I grieved for what could have been.

For my childhood I never got to share with him.

For the father-daughter bond that never had a chance to form.

For the moments I had imagined—the ones where he would tell me stories about his past, where I could hear his voice and know it was a part of me too, where I could see some reflection of myself in him.

Now, those moments would never come.

Grief isn't simple, and it's never just about the present.

Beneath the surface, another part of me stirred—one I thought I had buried.

The little girl who still lives deep inside of me in a hidden corner. She peeks out occasionally when I least expect her to, and that's when it can get interesting. The little girl curled up in a ball and sobbed as her heart broke into a million pieces. Her daddy was gone, and he was never going to be there. He was never going to be the man she needed him to be. Never going to be the daddy she wanted him to be.

Even though I had already spent years learning to live without him, his death brought it all back. I grieved Allen's death. I grieved that he was never the dad I wanted or needed growing up. I grieved all the missed opportunities. Through his absence, Allen had shaped my life; through his death, my life was again forever changed.

Just when I thought I had finally closed that chapter ... God was about to hand me the *truth*.

A truth that would shake everything I thought I knew. A truth that would change *everything*.

Field Notes:
Evidence for Healing

God often uses what we missed to show us what we're called to create.

REFLECTION QUESTIONS

- Have you ever walked into one role and found yourself called to something much bigger?

- What unexpected people has God used to bring healing into your life?

- How have second chances surprised you with joy you didn't see coming?

WRITING PROMPT

Write about a time something felt like a detour but turned out to be a divine appointment. What did it teach you? What doors opened from it?

ENCOURAGEMENT

God is a master at turning "temporary" into "transformational." That thing you think is just a stop along the way? It might be the very place He's planting your next season of joy. Don't underestimate small beginnings—they often hold big blessings.

SCRIPTURE ANCHOR

"God sets the lonely in families ..."

– Psalm 68:6a

PRAYER

God, thank You for the unexpected gifts that came from what I thought was just survival. Thank You for the people You bring into my life—especially the unexpected ones. Help me to trust that You see the whole picture, even when I'm just trying to hold it together one juice box at a time. Thank You for showing me that love can grow in the most ordinary places. Amen.

Unraveling Secrets: The Moment that Changed Everything

"Then you will know the truth, and the truth will set you free."
– John 8:32

Truth has a way of breaking chains, but it also has a way of breaking hearts. When I discovered Allen wasn't my father, everything I thought I knew about myself shifted in an instant. It was liberating—but also devastating.

Discovering the truth about my father wasn't just about facts or names—it was about the deep, soul-level impact of what that truth meant for me and my family. It was freeing, yes, but not without pain.

Life can change in the blink of an eye.

Everything you know, everything you love—it can all shift in a single moment.

One phone call.

A knock on the door.

A text.

That's all it takes, and suddenly, your well-ordered world is tossed into chaos. You're left to pick up the pieces, to begin again, unsure which way is up.

That's how it felt when the truth about Allen came to light. For most of my life, I believed that he was my father. It wasn't a question, a doubt, or even something I'd ever considered might be wrong. It was just ... fact. It was the foundation I built so much of my identity on. Who wouldn't?

Mom had always been honest with me—at least, that's what I believed. She made it clear that there were things people told her growing up that weren't true, and she promised me she wouldn't do the same. *"I want you to always know the truth,"* she said.

And I believed her, fully and without question.

But as much as the truth can set you free, it can also pull the rug right out from under you.

Remember I mentioned Allen's mother, Dorothy? I've always been fascinated with family trees. Maybe it was because I didn't know much about Allen's family, and I wanted to fill that hole. Whatever the reason, God used it.

He used it to bring a secret to light.

He used it to help heal a hole.

And He's still using it to repair a heart.

One night about fourteen years after Allen's death, I was working on my family tree, focusing on his mother's side. I knew her name and her sister's name, but that was it.

My research kept hitting dead ends.

I couldn't find anything else about them, their parents, or any ancestors. It was frustrating, and part of me started to wonder if I'd remembered her name wrong. After all, it wasn't like I'd ever met her—she was murdered long before I was even a thought. Then I remembered the papers Allen's grandmother Lola had given me years ago.

Lola had been a sweet, faith-filled woman who welcomed me into her family with open arms. Before she passed, she handed me all the documents she had about Allen.

It wasn't a lot, but it was enough.

That night, as I stared at my computer screen in frustration, something nudged me to dig out that old file.

Inside were pieces of Allen's story: His death certificate. His enlistment paperwork. His military discharge papers. A newspaper article about the time he'd gone to the Mayo Clinic as a child.

I sat there flipping through the documents, trying to see if anything would spark a lead for Dorothy's side of the family.

And that's when I saw it.

Have you ever looked closely at these kinds of forms?

They contain all sorts of information—Some of it mundane. Some of it incredibly personal. One detail stood out to me: *Allen's blood type.*

Blood type? I know—it seems like such a random thing to focus on, right? But that's exactly what God used to get my attention. When I stumbled across Allen's military paperwork that night, I wasn't looking for a bombshell. I was simply piecing together the family tree, trying to fill in gaps and understand more about Allen's side of the family.

I was sifting through his discharge papers, his birth certificate, whatever scraps of history I had. And then, there it was: blood type.

Mom's blood type is B positive.

Mine is O positive.

Allen's? AB positive.

I wasn't great at science in school, but even I knew enough about blood types to recognize the impossible when I saw it. There was no way Allen could be my biological father. I sat there staring at the document, my mind reeling. This wasn't just about biology; it was about everything I thought I knew about myself.

Who was I if not Allen's daughter?

And yet, even in the chaos, a quiet, steady voice whispered in my heart: "***He's not your father.***"

It wasn't loud or dramatic; it was calm and certain. I knew that voice.

It was God's.

The house was quiet, wrapped in the kind of stillness that only comes late at night when the world has settled. I sat alone in the dark study, the glow of the computer screen casting long shadows across the room. The hum of the hard drive was the only sound, a soft, rhythmic reminder that I wasn't dreaming.

Allen wasn't my birth father.

The realization settled over me, not like a crashing wave, but like a gentle tide pulling back to reveal something that had been there all along. I should have felt devastation, panic, even anger. But instead, there was peace—an unshakable calm that I couldn't explain. And beneath that, something even more surprising.

Relief.

A weight I hadn't even realized I was carrying was lifted, and in that moment, before the storm of emotions that would surely come later, my first reaction—crazily enough—was happiness. It didn't make sense, but it was real. For the first time in my life, I wasn't holding onto a question. I finally had an answer.

For a moment, relief washed over me. The man I'd spent years feeling disconnected from wasn't my father? A weight I didn't even realize I'd been carrying suddenly lifted. But almost immediately, the relief was replaced by a flood of questions, emotions, and uncertainty.

Before I called my mom, I needed to confirm what I suspected. No. What I knew in my heart and soul.

I picked up the phone and called the mother of one of my youngest son's classmates—A sweet woman who also happened to be an OB/GYN. As delicately as I could, I explained what I'd found and asked her if I was remembering high school biology correctly. She confirmed my suspicions: Given my mom's and my blood types, Allen couldn't possibly be my biological father.

Still, I needed further confirmation, so I turned to the trusty internet. A quick search solidified the truth I already knew in my heart.

Allen wasn't my father.

With that certainty in hand, I felt a mix of emotions swirling within me—

Relief

Confusion

A strange sense of anticipation

I couldn't wait to find out who my father truly was.

Armed with this knowledge, I knew I had to confront the one person who held the answers I so desperately needed—my mom.

So, I did what any confused and emotional daughter would do—I picked up the phone and called my mom.

I was laughing at this point. I know, you probably think I'm crazy for finding this discovery funny, but I really did—at first. Seriously, how could I not? I didn't grow up with Allen as my dad.

At that moment—I was happy that he's not my father.

And I couldn't wait to find out who it was!

Let me admit right here that I probably didn't handle this call as delicately as I could or should have. And that, my friend, is stating it mildly.

It was a Sunday evening when I picked up the phone, still a little nervous but oddly amused by the situation. When Mom answered, I didn't beat around the bush. "Who's my dad?" I asked, unable to hide the laughter in my voice. Her response was immediate, almost dismissive. "You know who your dad is."

"You're right," I said, correcting myself. "I mean, who's my biological father? It's not Allen. Who is it?" (You see I never called

Allen "Dad." He was always referred to as Father, sperm donor, birth father, etc. You get the idea.)

There was a pause on her end of the line—a long one.

When she finally spoke, her voice was strained. "Yes, it is. Allen is your father." I took a deep breath, trying to keep my tone calm as I explained. "Mom, it's not possible. I've done the research. His blood type was AB positive. Yours is B positive. Mine is O positive. It's biologically impossible for Allen to be my father."

Another pause. Then came her answer, defensive and firm: "The military must've gotten it wrong on his paperwork."

I couldn't help but sigh. "Mom, no. This isn't something the military would mess up. It's life-or-death information. Blood types aren't just randomly assigned." She didn't say much after that, and the conversation ended without any real answers.

But I wasn't about to give up. I figured she'd need some time to process everything, and I fully expected her to come over the next day ready to tell me the truth.

As I hung up the phone, a wave of emotions washed over me— confusion, anger, disbelief, and a deep ache that I couldn't quite name.

I sat there staring at the phone in my hand, as if it might suddenly give me the answers Mom refused to provide. My mind raced, replaying the conversation over and over, dissecting every word she had said, every pause, every strained note in her voice.

"The military must've gotten it wrong on his paperwork." Her words echoed in my head, and with each repetition, the disbelief grew.

It wasn't just that she denied the truth—It was that she reached for something so implausible, so absurd, as an explanation. The military? Getting a blood type wrong? This wasn't some clerical error on a form.

This was science.

Biology.

Life and death. How could she expect me to believe that?

I wanted to give her the benefit of the doubt. I wanted to believe that her defensiveness came from a place of shock, not deceit. But deep down, I knew better. This wasn't just about Allen or his blood type—This was about something bigger. Something she was desperately trying to keep buried.

The laughter that had bubbled in my voice when I asked the question was gone now, replaced by a hollow ache in my chest. I felt like a child again, standing on the edge of some great, unknowable truth, afraid to take the next step. The woman I had trusted implicitly—my mom, my best friend—had just denied the undeniable. And worse, she had tried to gaslight me into questioning what I knew to be true.

Why? Why wouldn't she tell me? What was she so afraid of? I felt my hands start to tremble, and I clenched them into fists, trying to steady myself. A knot formed in my stomach, tightening with each passing second.

The realization began to sink in: Mom wasn't going to make this easy. She wasn't going to hand me the answers I so desperately needed. If I wanted the truth, I was going to have to fight for it—dig for it—because she wasn't ready to give it to me.

But even as the anger simmered, there was an undercurrent of sadness. A deep, aching sadness that made my chest feel heavy. It hurt. It hurt to think that she had carried this secret for so long. That she had chosen to keep it from me, even when the truth was staring us both in the face.

What was it about me—about us—that made her think I couldn't handle it?

For a moment, the hurt transformed into something sharper—resentment.

How could she lie to me like this?

How could she let me believe something for my entire life, only to dismiss me when I questioned it?

Didn't she realize what this meant to me?

Didn't she see how much this mattered?

But then, just as quickly, the resentment softened.

Because I did know why.

I knew her well enough to understand that this wasn't about me. It was about her. Her shame. Her fear. Maybe even her guilt.

And as much as it hurt to admit, part of me felt sorry for her. Sorry that she had carried this burden alone for so many years. Sorry that she couldn't see how much better it would be to just let it go, to tell the truth.

I took a deep breath, letting it out slowly, trying to calm the storm inside me.

I wasn't done yet.

I couldn't be.

This was only the beginning.

But as I sat there in the quiet, the weight of the moment pressed down on me.

For the first time in my life, I felt the fragile threads of trust between us start to fray.

And I wondered. Would they ever be the same again? Could they be?

One thing was certain: I couldn't stop now.

The truth was out there, and I was going to find it. No matter how painful the journey, no matter how many walls I had to break down, I was going to get the answers I deserved. But for now, all I could do was wait and hope that, come tomorrow, she'd be ready to meet me halfway.

The next day came, and Mom did stop by, just as I'd anticipated. But to my surprise, there was no big revelation, no heartfelt confession. When I brought it up again, she stuck to her guns, insisting the military must have made a mistake. I pressed her gently, trying to coax out more information, but instead of answers, she pivoted to something I never saw coming. "Maybe you were switched at birth."

I blinked; certain I had misheard her. "What?"

"You were supposed to be a boy," she said, her voice trembling. "The whole pregnancy, the doctors told me I was having a boy. Maybe there was a mix-up at the hospital, and they gave me the wrong baby. How are we going to find your real parents?"

Her words hit like a freight train.

For a moment, I couldn't breathe. Was she serious? Did she actually believe this? And worse—was it possible?

The idea of being switched at birth was horrifying. If she were right, it would mean I'd lose everything: The family I'd grown up with. My grandparents, Granny and Granddaddy. My aunts and uncles.

My entire sense of identity.

The thought left me reeling.

But something deep inside me knew it wasn't true. It couldn't be. Yet, the fact was that she would rather cling to such an improbable scenario than admit the truth about Allen. That hurt more than I can put into words.

Her words cut deep, not just because of their absurdity, but because they revealed how far she was willing to go to avoid the truth. For the first time in my life, I felt like my mom—my best friend, my anchor—had chosen her secrets over me.

I was heartbroken. It felt like my whole world was unraveling. The mother I trusted more than anyone else was willing to let me believe I didn't belong—just to protect her secret.

For weeks, the weight of it all hung over me like a cloud. Mom and I talked, but the tension was undeniable. Every conversation felt like a delicate dance around the truth, and the longer it went on, the more the hurt festered.

Growing up, I always said that Mom was my best friend. We were very close.

I spoke with her on the phone multiple times a day, saw her a couple of times a week at minimum. We had always been close. Everyone said so. Until this.

I was happy Allen wasn't my sperm donor, as I would affectionately call him. It gave me the chance to have a decent man as my biological father. I mean, really—whoever he was had to be better, right? At that point, I hadn't thought of the potential ramifications. He could have been worse.

God opening my eyes was a wonderful blessing.

At the time, I didn't fully understand it. The revelation that Allen wasn't my birth father was shocking, painful even—but it was also an undeniable act of God's grace. He wasn't just giving me an answer; He was guiding me toward truth, toward healing, toward something far greater than I could have imagined.

For years, I had built a part of my identity around who I thought I was, around the story I had been told. But God, in His infinite wisdom, knew the truth all along. And when the time was right, He revealed it—not to hurt me, not to hurt my mom, but to free us both.

Because the truth does that—it sets us free.

God knew that I needed to let go of the weight of uncertainty, the silent questions that had lived in the back of my mind for so long. He knew that in showing me the truth, I would not only find my biological father but also discover something even deeper—His presence, His sovereignty, His perfect plan for my life.

What felt like loss at first was actually protection. What seemed like a painful revelation was really an invitation—an invitation to trust Him more fully, to surrender my need for control, and to walk in the assurance that He was writing a story far greater than I could ever pen myself.

In the end, it wasn't just about finding my birth father.

It was about finding *my Father*, the One who had been there all along.

But knowing the truth and being ready for the truth are two very different things.

At first, I was euphoric. I had answers! God had shown me what I had longed to know.

But then the weight of it settled in. The pain. The heartache. The unavoidable reality that this truth, while freeing, also had the power to shatter everything around me.

God knew what was coming—the storm that was about to tear through my world.

But I didn't.

I was, once again, that naive girl.

Not only was my world about to be rocked, but so were the lives of those I loved most—the people closest to me, the ones who had been there since the very beginning. Some already knew the truth. Some didn't. And me? I walked right into the middle of it all, cheerfully and without hesitation, and threw a hand grenade into my family.

I may have been 45 years old, but suddenly, I felt like a child again—naively opening a can of worms far bigger than I had ever anticipated.

And my mom.

I hurt her.

I forced her to face something she had spent decades burying, something she never imagined she'd have to admit out loud.

This book will possibly add to the hurt I've caused my mom. I don't want to hurt her, but I know that our story has the potential to help someone else. How do I know this? I've spoken with enough people over the last ten years who have amazingly similar stories. The fact that I was willing to be open about mine, and the hurt surrounding it, has helped them know that they weren't alone.

I sometimes think that I should have started writing back when I was living it. When it was raw and real. When I had to rely on God to get through the day. When there were days I'd stand in the kitchen, at the island, and cry because I hurt so much.

But I didn't.

Mom. I love her. I loved her then. I always have and always will. Remember I said I was happy to find out Allen wasn't my birth father? That's true, but there were many other emotions involved. I love my mom; we'd been close my whole life. But with this revelation, we hit a rocky patch.

How do you move forward from this? How do you cope with the realization that your mother has lied to you for 45 years? That she let you ...

Search for a man believing he's your father?
Build a relationship with a sweet old woman you believed was your great-grandmother?
Look for and find your supposed half-brother?
Bury a great-uncle, the great-grandmother, and the father you thought were yours?
Mourn all that could have been with your father?

These thoughts and more were bombarding my mind and this is where the pain, hurt, and anger started.

How would you feel if a massive secret about your conception suddenly came to light—and instead of telling the truth, your mother went with the *switched at birth* excuse?

Let me just say, it sucks.

Knowing that she would rather rewrite my entire existence than admit the truth hurt. That she would rather I question everything about myself than face what really happened. That even 45 years later, her secret was more important than me—her daughter.

Don't get me wrong, I didn't expect it to be easy for her. I didn't expect her to just come out and say it.

I had already run through every possible scenario in my head. Every way this could have happened. Because let's be real, I never imagined my parents were perfect. And I was born in 1968.

Several possibilities had crossed my mind: a one-night stand where she didn't know his name, an affair with a married man, rape, or something else I hadn't even considered.

But here's the thing—I didn't care.

Well ... maybe I cared. But not in the way you'd think.

I cared because it had obviously been a painful time for her. I cared because something had happened that she had spent decades trying to bury. But for me?

I didn't care.

God was there.

He was there before my mother even knew I existed.

He was the One who formed me, who gave me life, who knew every detail about me before I ever took a breath. My story didn't start with my mother's choices or my father's absence—it started with God's plan.

> "*For you created my inmost being; you knit me together in my mother's womb. I praise you because I am fearfully and wonderfully made; your works are wonderful, I know that full well.*" (Psalm 139:13-14)

I wasn't an accident. I wasn't a mistake. I wasn't an unwanted consequence.

I was created with intention, with love, with purpose.

Whatever happened, however I came to be, I know this—I wouldn't be here if He didn't have a purpose for me.

And **THAT** truth? It outweighs everything else.

After Mom suggested I might have been switched at birth, her words carried such heartfelt emotion and sorrow that it shook me. She grieved, wondering aloud how she could not have realized I wasn't her birth child. And as much as I tried to dismiss it, a tiny part of me wondered too.

What if she were right?

What if I had been switched?

What was I going to do? I did what any frustrated detective would do—I got to work. First, I needed Mom's DNA.

How, you ask?

Simple: I told her that since I didn't know who my father was, I needed her DNA to figure out which portion of my ancestry came from him. Which was true ... but I also needed it to confirm if she was, in fact, my mother.

I sent her sample off to **Ancestry.com** and waited. It was one of the longest waits of my life, every passing day filled with "what ifs." When the email came through, I stared at it for what felt like hours, too scared to open it. What if the results upended my life even more?

When I finally clicked, the words "parental match" jumped out at me, and I exhaled a breath I didn't realize I was holding. She was my mom. Despite everything, that truth remains unshaken.

The confirmation brought instant relief: Yes, she was my mom. I didn't have to search for a whole new set of parents. I wasn't switched at birth.

I was just back to looking for my dad—again.

The truth had set me free, but not in the way I expected. It freed me from a false narrative, from a story I'd unknowingly clung to for decades. But freedom doesn't come without a cost—and my heart bore the weight of it.

In fact, the night I finally confronted her about this train she was on, I hit my lowest point. And in the process, I discovered how wonderful my two oldest sons are and how blessed I am to be their mother.

My husband, Chuck, was out of town. My oldest son, Charlie, was 21 and home from college for the weekend, while Spencer, my 16-year-old, was still in high school. That night, I had just returned from a school function for the kids, and the parking lot had become the scene of my emotional unraveling. I was angry, heartbroken, and frustrated. I had told my mom how much it hurt that she would rather I believe I wasn't her daughter than admit Allen wasn't my father—and tell me who was. The weight of her avoidance, her refusal to face the truth, pressed down on me, and I felt like I was suffocating.

When I got home, the house was a mixture of noise and quiet. The boys had a few friends over, the younger kids were asleep, and it was close to midnight. But I was in pieces. I needed someone—anyone—to remind me I wasn't alone, to physically show me they cared. I needed the tangible, comforting arms of God in that moment, through the people I loved most.

I stayed in my room for a while, trying to pull myself together, but the ache was too much. Finally, I opened the door, walked to the edge of the living room, and called out, "I need a hug."

My voice must have betrayed just how much I was hurting because, within seconds, both Charlie and Spencer were standing there. Without hesitation, they wrapped their arms around me, and I broke down completely. Tears poured down my face, my body shaking as sobs wracked through me. My breath came in short, uneven gasps, my chest rising and falling with years of bottled-up pain. My fingers clenched their shirts, gripping them like a lifeline, as if letting go would mean falling apart completely. And in that moment, I did—I let go. Not of them, but of everything I had been holding inside. The weight of questions, grief, and unspoken heartache spilled out in a flood of trembling shoulders and tear-streaked cheeks. I wasn't just crying—I was releasing, unraveling, finally allowing myself to feel it all.

I don't know how long we stood there like that—me sobbing, them holding me—but in that moment, I felt the kind of love and reassurance I desperately needed. My sons, my sweet boys, were the physical embodiment of God's comfort. They were His arms, His presence, His love, carrying me through the storm.

In their embrace, I felt something shift. Their love reminded me that no matter how messy life became, I wasn't alone. God had placed these incredible young men in my life as a reminder of His unwavering presence.

That night was a turning point for me. Up until then, I had approached everything with a kind of detached curiosity—like it was just a puzzle to be solved. But standing there, surrounded by my sons' love and support, something shifted. This wasn't a game. It wasn't just about uncovering facts or filling in blanks on a family tree. It was real. Messy. Painful. And for the first time, I allowed myself to feel the full weight of it—not just what I had lost, but what I might still find.

In the weeks that followed, I struggled with anger and disappointment. But God gently reminded me that forgiveness wasn't just for her. It was for me, too.

The power of forgiveness. Forgiveness meant: releasing the pain, making room for healing, and trusting Him to mend what felt irreparably broken.

As I've said, Mom and I have always been close. Like, really close. When I was little, we did everything together, and I could talk to her about anything. It was great. Even as a teenager—most of the time, anyway—I could still go to her with stuff. But let's be real—there were those rare occasions when I didn't exactly want to share everything. Problem was that she always knew if I wasn't telling the truth. I'm convinced God tattled on me.

Take, for instance, the infamous Greenspoint Mall incident. I was a senior in high school, and my friend Angel and I decided we had to go shoe shopping for our senior prom. Greenspoint Mall—known affectionately (or not-so-affectionately) as Gunspoint—was about an hour from Conroe. Totally worth it for the perfect pair of shoes, right?

Wrong. Mom wasn't having it. She flat-out told me no, saying there were plenty of stores in Conroe to find what I needed.

Did I listen? Of course not. I was 18 and determined to show her just how wrong she was.

So, Angel and I went on our great Greenspoint adventure. Hours of mall wandering, and guess what? Nothing. Not a single pair of shoes that worked. Frustrated, we drove back to Conroe and—wouldn't you know it? The first store we walked into had the exact shoes we'd been hunting for. The exact ones. Mom was right. (Yes, Mom, I said it. You were right.)

Feeling triumphant about the shoes but guilty about the trip, I got home and tried to act like everything was fine. Mom asked casually, "Did you go to the mall?" "Nope." I said it, all cool and confident. She asked again, and I stuck to my story. Finally, she dropped the hammer: "Before you left, God told me to write down your car's mileage. You have too many miles for someone who just shopped in Conroe."

Busted. Thanks, God. Tattletale.

My punishment? A month-long grounding. No car to drive to school. Had to ride the bus unless I could hitch a ride with a friend. Spent the last stretch of senior year grounded.

Lesson learned. (Well, sort of.)

As life moved on, and I grew up, got married, and started my own family, Mom and I stayed just as close. We talked on the phone several times a day, went to lunch, and hit the shops together (with fewer restrictions). She'd watch my kids when I had classes or traveled, and she was always there when I needed her.

Always.

I trusted her completely—Why wouldn't I? She was my mom.

Field Notes:
Evidence for Healing

God's truth untangles the deepest lies and brings clarity where confusion once reigned.

REFLECTION QUESTIONS

- Has a truth ever changed everything you thought you knew?
- How do you process denial—especially from someone close to you?
- What helps you stay grounded when the story you've always been told no longer adds up?

ENCOURAGEMENT

Truth can feel like both a scalpel and a salve. It cuts, but it also begins the healing. Even when others try to bury it, God is in the business of uncovering what needs to be brought into the light. And no matter what you find, you are still loved, still chosen, still His.

WRITING PROMPT

Write about a moment when you began to question a version of the story you were told. How did you begin to separate fact from fiction? What gave you the strength to keep digging?

SCRIPTURE ANCHOR

"For God is not a God of disorder but of peace."

– 1 Corinthians 14:33

PRAYER

Father, You see what's hidden and love me anyway. When truth feels heavy, help me carry it. When denial stings, steady me in Your peace. Give me wisdom to hold what's mine and release what's not. Thank You for meeting me in the mess and never letting go. Amen.

CASE FILE #008

Healing in His Presence

"The LORD is close to the brokenhearted and saves those who are crushed in spirit."
– Psalm 34:18

Still tender from my breakdown with the boys just a couple of months earlier, I went to a women's retreat with a local church—unsure of what I was looking for, but knowing I needed something. It wasn't the church where I was currently a member, but I knew a few of the ladies there and felt like God was nudging me to go. He just kept whispering that it would be good for me, so I signed up. I arrived at the retreat with a mix of nervousness and hope, unsure of what God had in store for me. Little did I know, He was about to meet me in ways I couldn't have imagined.

Now, let me paint you a picture: I'm naturally a shy, introverted homebody. I'll admit it—I wasn't exactly thrilled about stepping out of my comfort zone. Sharing a room with strangers? Not my idea of a good time.

But sometimes, God has a way of pushing us toward what we need, even if it's not what we want. Talk about nerve-wracking!

But God?

Oh, He knew exactly what I needed. Walking into that retreat, I carried more than just my overnight bag—I carried exhaustion, unspoken burdens, and a heart that felt both heavy and guarded. But God, in His perfect way, placed me in a room with three incredible women who would become more than just roommates for the weekend. He knew I needed their laughter to break through my weariness, their kindness to remind me I wasn't alone, and their prayers to cover the parts of my heart I wasn't ready to share. Through conversations late into the night, quiet moments of reflection, and the simple comfort of sisterhood, I felt His presence weaving through it all. It wasn't just a retreat—it was a divine appointment.

From the moment I arrived, it was clear that He had orchestrated every detail. My roommates turned out to be gentle, kind, joyful and so full of grace. They were exactly what my hurting heart needed.

And that weekend?

It became one of the most powerful encounters with God I've ever had.

During the first session, a lady I've known since I was a young teen approached me with an expression of awe and urgency. She told me she'd seen a vision—and her words painted a picture so vivid, I could almost see it myself.

She described Niagara Falls—mighty and unrelenting. Water cascading with a force that left no stone untouched, massive boulders surrounding me, water gushing out from every direction, crashing with a roar that could drown out any voice

Yet there I was, standing in the middle of it all, steady in the chaos.

Then she said something I'll never forget: **"God wants you to crawl into His lap, curl up, and let Him hold you close."** In that moment, her words felt like an invitation—Not just to surrender, but to finally find the rest I'd been searching for.

The crashing water of the falls mirrored the chaos inside me— each wave pounding against my heart, relentless and unyielding. But even as the storm raged, there was an unshakable truth: I wasn't standing alone. The vision reflected my reality—the pain of rejection, the ache of loss, the weight of unanswered questions, the sheer exhaustion of holding it all together.

The sound of the falls, deafening and constant, reminded me of the noise in my own mind—the "what-ifs" and "whys" that never stopped swirling, demanding answers I didn't have.

Then there were the boulders I was standing amongst—huge. Immovable. Unyielding. They were the obstacles I'd faced for as long as I could remember: the lies I didn't know were lies, the missing pieces of my identity, the relationships that felt just out of reach.

Each boulder represented something I couldn't fix, something I couldn't change, no matter how hard I tried. They surrounded me in the vision, making me feel small and powerless. But even as the water rushed and crashed, the boulders stayed firm—almost as if they were holding me in place.

Then came the part that left me undone: *Crawling into God's lap.*

Just the thought of it brought a flood of emotions. For so long, I'd carried the weight of my own pain, trying to figure out where I belonged and who I was. The idea of surrendering all of that, of resting in the safety of God's embrace, felt both foreign and desperately needed.

In the vision, crawling into God's lap wasn't just an act of surrender. It was a homecoming!

It was the kind of safety I'd been searching for my whole life. There, in His lap, I wasn't just loved—I was **cherished**. I wasn't just comforted—I was **healed**.

The crashing water couldn't reach me. The noise was silenced, the chaos stilled.

And for the first time in what felt like forever, I felt protected. Safe. Held.

At that moment, I realized the vision wasn't about escaping the water or avoiding the boulders. It was about trusting God to carry me through it all. The water might keep rushing. The boulders might never move. But in His lap, I was steady. I was loved. And I was enough.

As the weekend unfolded, God continued to meet me in unexpected ways. From the vision of Niagara Falls to the powerful moments of worship, His presence was undeniable.

The room was dimly lit, the soft glow of string lights casting gentle shadows on the walls. Music filled the air—rich, layered, and reverent. It wasn't just something I heard; I **felt** it. The bass reverberated through the floor, each beat thrumming in my chest like a second heartbeat. The voices, rising and falling in harmony, wrapped around me like a wave, swelling higher and higher, drawing me in. It was powerful, almost overwhelming, like standing at the edge of the ocean and feeling the tide pull at my feet.

As the music built, it felt like my soul was opening up, each note reaching into the deepest parts of me, places I hadn't even realized were still locked away. Singing wasn't just worship—it was a release, a surrender, a way to pour out everything I'd been holding in. The weight of my unanswered questions, my silent prayers, and my aching heart spilled out with every lyric.

I stood there, hands lifted high, my face tilted toward the ceiling, eyes closed against the world around me. The warmth of the moment wrapped around me like a blanket—gentle, yet undeniable. My heart pounded, raw and vulnerable, aching with questions I had carried for so long. Would I ever have an answer? Did God see me? Was I truly known?

I began to sing, my voice mingling with the others, yet feeling intensely personal—like this was a moment crafted just for me. Each word felt like a prayer I didn't know I needed, like an offering being lifted to heaven. And as I surrendered, the presence of God enveloped me, steady, unshakable, and more real than anything I had ever known.

Then, it happened.

At first, it was subtle—a soft warmth at the top of my head, so faint I almost didn't notice. It was like the brush of a sunbeam filtering through a window, delicate and fleeting. But as I kept singing, as I let my heart open wider, it grew.

The warmth thickened, spreading slowly, deliberately, like honey spilled from an urn—golden, rich, and all-encompassing. It oozed over me with a gentle weight, sinking deep into my skin, pressing into every aching part of me. It wasn't just warmth; it was something far greater.

Peace. A peace that silenced every lingering doubt, wrapping around me like a whisper from heaven itself. Assurance. A knowing, a certainty that I was seen, that I was known, that I was held. Love. A love so complete, so overwhelming, that it seeped into the cracks of my brokenness and made them whole.

In my mind's eye, I saw it clearly—a large urn, suspended above me, tilted just enough to pour out its contents. It wasn't a trick of my imagination. It was real. As though heaven itself had opened, spilling anointing oil, a divine outpouring meant just for me.

My breath caught in my throat. My shoulders, tight with years of carrying the weight of my questions, began to relax. My chest, heavy with longing, suddenly felt light. My heart, once aching with the emptiness of searching, filled with something far greater than I had expected. Tears slipped down my cheeks, unbidden, unstoppable. But they weren't just tears of longing anymore—they were tears of release, of surrender, of knowing I was in the presence of the One who had been with me all along.

Then, through the stillness of my heart, I heard it.

A voice, gentle yet unmistakable. Close enough to feel like a whisper, yet powerful enough to shake me to my core.

"This is My oil I am pouring out over you."

The words weren't just spoken; they were etched onto my heart, settled into my spirit in a way that left no room for doubt. I stood there, letting it all soak in—every drop of His presence, every ounce of His love.

And for the first time in what felt like forever, I wasn't just searching. I was found.

The words were so clear, so intimate, they felt as though they were etched directly onto my heart. I stood there, letting it all soak in. For the first time in what seemed like forever, I felt whole. Not perfect, not without questions, but whole in God's presence. I wish I could remember everything else He said (note of advice: always write these things down!), but the feeling of being completely covered in His love has stayed with me ever since.

As I stood there, soaking in this incredible moment, a woman I had just met that day reached over and placed her hand on my head. She leaned in and said, "I can feel the Holy Spirit all over you. He's pouring His oil over you." Then she added words that sent chills through me: "He has your answer, and it's coming—in His time."

My answer.

The very question I had been begging God to answer for what felt like forever. I wanted to know who my father was. This was the one thing I had been searching for my whole life—the missing piece that left me feeling incomplete.

I wanted to know. I needed to know. I was hurting so deeply; it felt like I was breaking apart. My heart ached in ways I didn't know were possible, and I couldn't imagine a day when it wouldn't.

But in that moment, I felt a glimmer of hope. God was there, holding me together, whispering promises over me. And I held on, trusting that He was guiding me toward the answer I so desperately longed for. When the woman said, "He has your answer, and it's coming—in His time," my heart swelled with hope. God had my answer. It was coming. But as much as I wanted to believe those words, I felt the familiar tug of impatience gnawing at the edges of my heart. Waiting on God's timing? That sounded so noble in theory, but in practice? It was hard. So very hard.

God's timing is rarely easy to accept. But as I stood there in worship, I realized something: His timing isn't just about answers—it's about transformation. In the waiting, He was changing me, preparing me for the truth in ways I couldn't yet understand.

I wanted answers now. I had already spent what felt like a lifetime searching for my father, trying to piece together who I was and where I came from. Hearing that I had to wait even longer was like telling a child that Christmas morning had been postponed indefinitely. The ache of longing and the sting of uncertainty didn't vanish just because someone promised they'd be resolved eventually. The promise of "in His time" was comforting, sure—but it wasn't easy.

I wrestled with God in the quiet moments. Why not now, Lord? You have the answers. You know the way. Why can't I just have it already? It wasn't that I didn't trust Him—I did. I believed He would bring the answer when the time was right. But the waiting? It stretched me in ways I didn't think I could endure. Every day felt like a small eternity. Every silence felt deafening. Every delay felt like a weight pressing on my chest.

At the same time, deep in my spirit, I knew: This waiting wasn't wasted. God was working in me, preparing me in ways I couldn't yet see. It's just that sometimes I wanted to shout, "Can we please fast-forward to the part where everything makes sense?"

Waiting on God's timing is one of the most beautiful paradoxes of faith. It's simultaneously an act of trust and a test of patience. It's learning to say, "I believe You know what's best," even when every fiber of your being wants to grab the wheel and drive. It's leaning into His promise, even when it feels like nothing is happening.

In my heart, I knew this was a lesson I needed to learn—a lesson in trust. A lesson in letting go of control. A lesson in believing that God's plan was far better than anything I could orchestrate on my own.

But knowing that didn't make it any less frustrating.

So, I waited. I prayed. I cried. I wrestled. Waiting felt like a test I wasn't ready for. I wanted answers now, not later. I wrestled with God in those quiet moments, asking Him why the waiting had to be so hard. And through it all, I clung to the promise that He had my answer. Even when impatience threatened to overtake me, I held onto the truth that His timing, no matter how incomprehensible, was perfect.

In those moments of mixed acceptance, I began to realize that God had been quietly filling the spaces left empty by others. Each time I felt out of place, He reminded me of a deeper belonging—one that wasn't based on blood but on His love. God's presence was there all along, a steady foundation as I searched for answers, giving me a sense of family that couldn't be shaken by anyone's judgment.

That weekend didn't give me all the answers I was looking for, but it gave me something even more valuable: peace. The Lord truly is close to the brokenhearted. That weekend, He reminded me that healing doesn't always come with immediate answers. It begins in His presence. It reminded me that I wasn't alone, that God was with me every step of the way, even when the path felt uncertain. It was the first time I truly began to believe that healing didn't have to wait for the final answer. It could begin now, in His presence. And so, with my heart a little lighter and my hope renewed, I left that retreat ready to keep trusting, keep waiting, and keep believing that His plan for me—whatever it held—was good.

If you've ever felt overwhelmed by life's chaos, I want you to know this: God is there. In the middle of the crashing waves and unmovable boulders, He's waiting for you to rest in His arms. The answer might not come immediately, but His presence will sustain you.

Wherever you are in your own journey—whether you're waiting for answers, grieving a loss, or simply trying to make sense of life—know this: God is near. He's not just watching from a distance—He's right there with you, ready to pour His love over you. Sometimes you need to just climb in His lap and let His loving arms surround you. All you need to do is say yes to His invitation.

Field Notes:
Evidence for Healing

Healing doesn't erase the past; it redeems it.

REFLECTION QUESTIONS

- Have you ever had a moment where God's presence felt so real it was almost tangible?

- What physical or emotional signs has He used to let you know He's near?

- What does healing look like for you—not just spiritually, but emotionally or relationally?

ENCOURAGEMENT

God doesn't just patch the wound—He anoints it. His presence is thick, tender, and personal. He knows how to reach your heart in the way you'll understand it most. Don't underestimate the moments that feel quiet but holy. That's often where the deepest healing begins.

WRITING PROMPT

Describe a time when God met you in an unexpected way—through worship, prayer, or a word from someone else. What did it show you about His nearness? About your worth?

SCRIPTURE ANCHOR

"He heals the brokenhearted and binds up their wounds." – **Psalm 147:3**

PRAYER

Father, You see the wounds I've hidden and the ones I don't have words for. Thank You for meeting me in unexpected places and pouring out healing in ways I couldn't have imagined. Help me rest in Your presence and receive the restoration only You can give. Amen.

The DNA Trail: Following the Path to My Answers

"but those who hope in the LORD will renew their strength. They will soar on wings like eagles; they will run and not grow weary, they will walk and not be faint."
– Isaiah 40:31

I've always loved a good detective story and even dreamed of joining the CIA one day. So, when life handed me a real-life mystery—with sky-high stakes—I couldn't resist diving in headfirst. The mission? Find my biological father.

But this wasn't just about solving a puzzle; it was about finding the missing piece of me. Every question I asked, every lead I chased, felt like uncovering a chapter of my own story. Without knowing where I came from, it felt like living in a book with no ending—a story missing its final, all-important pages.

Starting this search was daunting—like trying to solve a mystery with no clues, no map, and a magnifying glass swiped from the bottom of a cereal box. The kind that was supposed to help you decode secret messages but mostly just made everything blurry. That's what this felt like—blurred, frustrating, impossible.

Every journey begins with a first step—or in my case, a desperate leap fueled by questions I couldn't ignore. My search for my father wasn't just about finding a name or a face. It was about uncovering the missing pieces of who I was.

Dad was amazing in his support of my search for my biological father. He understood my need to find out anything I could—who he was, where I came from, what family I belonged to. He got it. He knew that I felt like there was a hole inside me, a missing piece I couldn't quite fill.

But even with all of Dad's love and unwavering support, the question of my biological father never stopped tugging at me. It was always there, lingering in the background, waiting for answers.

What did he look like?

Did I have his eyes? His laugh?

Would he want to know me, or would I just be a stranger dredging up a past he'd rather forget?

These questions swirled in my mind, keeping me awake at night and pushing me forward during the day.

This wasn't just about finding a name or a face. It was about uncovering a piece of myself I'd always felt was missing. And if I didn't find him, I wasn't sure how I'd fill that empty space in my heart.

But hey, I'd always been stubborn.

If anyone could figure this out, it was me.

Right?

At least, that's what I told myself.

But the truth?

Truthfully, I didn't know where to start. Every lead felt like a dead end before I even took the first step. Every question I asked seemed to open a dozen more, none of them leading to answers that made sense. The weight of it pressed down on me. What if I was chasing something I would never find? What if the truth was buried too deep, locked away in the past with no one left to tell it?

Still, I couldn't shake the feeling that I had to keep going.

I'd spent my whole life carrying a question that had no answer. A blank space where a name should have been. A hole in my identity that no amount of pretending could fill. I had learned to live with it, to tuck it away neatly, convincing myself that it didn't matter as much as it did.

But it did matter.

It mattered more than I wanted to admit.

Because knowing where we come from matters.

And if the truth was out there, I was going to find it. Even if it meant digging through old records, pestering relatives for stories they didn't want to tell, and searching through scraps of memories that didn't feel like mine.

Even if it meant facing things I wasn't sure I was ready to face.

I had no idea what I would find. I had no way of knowing how much this journey would change me. But one thing was certain— this wasn't just about a name. It was about knowing the truth, no matter what it cost.

And I was ready to find it.

Looking back now, I realize that God was nudging me toward this search long before I took the first step. At the time, I thought it was just my own curiosity or a longing to fill that empty space in my heart. But now, I see it was His plan all along—gently preparing me for the road ahead.

Let me just say, this wasn't exactly *Mission: Impossible*, but it wasn't a walk in the park either. I had scraps of information—a few names, a blurry timeline, and a heap of unanswered questions.

It felt like trying to piece together a puzzle with half the pieces missing.

But I was determined, and I wasn't about to give up, not now.

Not when the questions still burned inside me. Not when I had spent my whole life wondering. Not when I could feel the truth hovering just beyond my reach, taunting me like a shadow that disappeared every time I got close enough to touch it.

So, I kept going.

I chased down every lead, even when it felt like I was running in circles. I pored over old records, my eyes blurring as I scrolled through page after page of handwritten documents, hoping—praying—that one of them would hold a name, a date, a clue that would bring me closer. Every night, I'd tell myself, *just five more minutes,* but those minutes always stretched into hours.

I asked questions. And then I asked them again. And again. I knew I was annoying people—family members, distant relatives, anyone who might know something. Some dodged my questions. Some gave me vague answers, half-truths wrapped in hesitation. But I didn't let that stop me. If they weren't ready to tell me, fine. I'd find another way.

I learned to pay attention to the small things—the shift in someone's voice, the way their eyes flickered just a little too fast when I asked a direct question. I started picking up on the gaps, the contradictions, the things that didn't quite add up. I wasn't just searching for the truth; I was piecing together a puzzle that had been scattered long before I was born.

There were nights when exhaustion begged me to stop. When the trail felt cold, and doubt crept in, whispering, *maybe you're not supposed to know. Maybe this is just how the story ends.* But I refused to believe that.

Because God didn't put this longing in my heart for nothing.

So, I prayed. Sometimes through clenched teeth. Sometimes through tears. Sometimes just a single word whispered into the silence: *Help.*

And somehow, He always did.

Just when I thought I had hit a dead end, something would happen. A forgotten memory would surface in a conversation. A document I'd overlooked would suddenly hold a detail I hadn't noticed before. A door would open when I least expected it.

But just as often, the resistance came.

People told me to let it go. That some things were better left buried. That I'd never find the truth, and even if I did, it wouldn't change anything.

But they didn't understand.

This wasn't about curiosity. This wasn't about proving a point. This was about *who I was*. And I wasn't stopping until I found the missing piece of my story.

The idea of what I might uncover made my stomach churn. What if he didn't want to be found? What if he was angry or rejected me outright? What if I found out things I wasn't ready to know? There were so many what-ifs swirling around in my head that it almost felt easier to just stay put, to let the questions simmer unanswered.

But that wasn't me. *I had to know.*

There was this ache inside me—a missing piece of who I was that I couldn't ignore anymore. I wanted answers. I needed them. Even if it meant facing hard truths or stumbling through the process blind, I was determined to try.

After all, wasn't it better to know than to keep living with the questions?

I asked questions. I made phone calls. I poked around, hoping someone—anyone—might have a clue.

My mom wasn't much help; her answers were vague, inconsistent at best, frustrating at worst. But I kept at it. Every lead, every scrap of information, was like a breadcrumb leading me closer to the truth—or so I hoped.

At the time, it felt like searching for a needle in a haystack, but with the added fear that the needle might not even exist. Still, I pressed on, because deep down, I believed that the answers were out there somewhere, waiting for me to find them.

I'll leave out some of the more mundane details—trust me, you're not missing much.

The important thing is that I had no idea where this journey would lead me or what I'd find along the way. What I did know was this: the search had begun, and there was no turning back.

Mom didn't give me his name—which, as frustrating as it was, also meant I got the chance to play detective.

But let's be real. I didn't want to play detective. I didn't want to piece together scraps of information, read between the lines, or sift through half-truths. I wanted a straight answer. A name. Something solid to hold on to.

And so, I asked.

It was just the two of us. I had been waiting for the right moment, that perfect window where she'd be relaxed, maybe even willing to open up. I don't know why I thought it would be easy. I took a deep breath, my fingers fidgeting with a loose thread on my sleeve. *Okay, here goes nothing.*

"Mom," I started, keeping my voice light but steady, "who is my father?"

She didn't look at me right away. Her hands were busy folding a dish towel, smoothing it over the counter, moving like she hadn't heard me. I knew she had. I waited, my stomach tightening with the silence. When she finally spoke, her voice was even, almost too even. "Why are you asking me that?"

I shrugged, like it wasn't a big deal. Like I wasn't hanging on her every word. "I just want to know." She sighed, still not meeting my eyes. "You already know."

That's when I knew this wasn't going to be a conversation. It was going to be a fight for the truth.

I forced a small laugh, trying to keep it casual, though my heart was pounding. "Do I, though?"

She finally looked at me then, her expression unreadable. "What do you mean?"

I hesitated for a second, but I had already come this far. "I mean, I know what you told me. But ... I just don't think that's the whole story."

Silence stretched between us, thick and heavy. I felt the tension settle in my chest. She looked away again. "It doesn't matter."

But it did matter.

I could feel frustration bubbling up, but I swallowed it down. I had to be careful. If I pushed too hard, she'd shut down completely. So, I tried again. Softer. "Mom, please. I just want the truth."

Another long pause. And then, finally— "I can't tell you."

My breath caught. My heart sank.

Not *won't* tell me. *Can't.*

That one word felt heavier than anything else she had said. It wasn't just avoidance. It was something more. Fear? Guilt? A secret so big she didn't know how to say it out loud? I searched her face, looking for something—anything—that would give me a clue. But she was a locked door, and I didn't have the key.

The frustration in me flared again. "You can't tell me? Or you *won't* tell me?"

She sighed again, rubbing her temples. "It's complicated."

I almost laughed. Complicated? That was an understatement.

But the truth was, I could feel it—she wasn't going to give me the answer I wanted. At least, not yet.

Still, I wasn't done searching.

If she wouldn't tell me, I'd find out myself.

And I had no idea just how deep this mystery would go.

The clues she did give me? He was blonde. He had blue eyes. He was in the military. Hmmm. Blonde hair and blue eyes? Check—I fit that description. Military? Okay, that tracks. At the time I was conceived, Mom was living in Glasgow, Montana, near an Air Force base. It seemed pretty safe to assume he was in the Air Force. Makes sense, right? But beyond that? Nothing. Not a name. Not a hint. Not even a breadcrumb to follow. Just those few little details to fuel a mystery that was starting to feel like it belonged in one of the novels I loved so much.

Where to start my search?

I started asking questions, trying to piece it all together. Why on earth did she move to Montana—and in December of all months? Seriously, who leaves Texas for Montana in the dead of winter? Don't get me wrong, Montana is stunning, but it's also freezing! But Texas? Warm, sunny, and full of family. Oh wait. I did leave Texas myself. Okay, scratch that question, and let's move on.

Still, it didn't add up.

All of Mom's family was in Texas, Louisiana, or Missouri. So, what was the draw to Glasgow, Montana? Did she know someone there? How did she end up meeting Allen? For those who don't know, Glasgow, Montana, had an Air Force base back then. And, as it turns out, Allen was stationed there when Mom met him.

Piecing these details together felt like unraveling clues in a mystery novel. Mom told me about moving to Montana, who she stayed with, and how she first met Allen. Apparently, it happened at a gas station near the base—back in the days when gas stations were full-service. She pulled in for gas, and Allen was the one who came out to fill her tank. I can only imagine how that first interaction went. Whatever he said must have worked, because soon after, they connected.

By May, Mom was five months pregnant with me, and they married. By October, when I arrived, they'd already left Montana for Texas, after Allen was transferred to Randolph Air Force Base in San Antonio.

One of the more memorable stories I grew up hearing about Allen was the one surrounding my birth. I was born in Channelview, Texas, where my grandparents and other relatives lived. Apparently, it took my Granddaddy and uncles three whole days to track Allen down. And where did they finally find him? Drunk in a bar. Yep. That right there gives you a pretty solid preview of the kind of man he was—or at least the version of him that story paints.

It wasn't going to be easy. For every answer I thought I'd found, there were ten more questions waiting to trip me up. But that didn't matter—I was determined to keep going, no matter where the road led.

When I started asking questions, I naturally turned to my family, hoping they might hold some answers. Their reactions? All over the map. Some were supportive. Some were shocked. And a few made it painfully clear that they thought I should leave it alone.

Unfortunately, the first people I would have gone to for insight—Granny and Granddaddy—were no longer around. Granddaddy passed away in August 1981. Granny followed on December 26, 2009. My uncle David Smith, who would have been only 13 when I was born, and likely didn't know much, had also passed away, in a tragic motorcycle accident, on December 7, 2003.

But there were still plenty of people I could bombard with my endless questions. And trust me, I did.

The responses I got? Some were surprised, others shocked, and then there were those who hit me with: "It's about time you realized and started asking questions."

Excuse me—*what?!* There was a question to be asked? Why didn't anyone clue me in?! And of course, there were the ones who said, "It's none of your business. Leave it alone. If she wanted you to know, she'd have told you by now." None of my business? Are you kidding me? This is most definitely my business! There's the medical side of it. The emotional side of it. Oh yes, it's my business, alright!

But either they didn't know who it was, or if they did, they weren't saying. For the first few weeks, I pieced together what I could from family and friends, digging for any scrap of information.

It didn't take long to hit a wall, though—and let me tell you—it was frustrating.

Would you like to know how deep I dug? Sure, I started with family and friends. But I didn't stop there—not even close. I tracked down Mom's high school boyfriend, thinking maybe he had some insight. It felt like something straight out of a detective novel—one of those moments where the protagonist is on the verge of cracking the case. Except this wasn't fiction. This was my life.

When I spoke with her old flame—let's call him Mason— he had me on speakerphone with his wife there, and his very first question caught me off guard: "When were you born? What's your birthday?" There was a pause, like he was doing the math in his head, and then came the bombshell: "Okay, I'm not your father."

Oh! That hadn't even crossed my mind! I wasn't expecting that. I was only reaching out to him because Mom said she'd moved to Montana at his brother's urging, and I thought maybe his brother might know something.

Mason went on to share his side of the story about that long-ago December when Mom left for Montana. It was fascinating to hear it from his perspective, after only knowing Mom's version of events. He went on to tell me about his brother's life—and his death. I felt a pang of sadness hearing it, for multiple reasons. Some, I admit, were selfish. There was a sense of loss, not just for Johnny, but for the answers I might never get.

He told me about the day he skipped school to take his brother Johnny to the train station. Johnny had been home on leave from the Air Force, back in town for a family member's funeral. Apparently, while Johnny was home, he had started falling for my mom, despite being married. That, as you can imagine, caused some tension between the brothers. At this point, Mason's wife chimed in: "I've heard stories about your mom for our entire marriage." Johnny and Mason had both cared deeply for her. Possibly even loved her.

Mason was kind enough to give me Johnny's widow's name and contact information. Now, before you think I'm some kind of heartless witch who reached out with, "Hey! I might be your late husband's daughter!"—Well, okay, I did. But in my defense, they weren't married when I was conceived. Still, not exactly the kind of letter anyone wants to receive.

To her credit, she was gracious. She actually called me, and we ended up talking on the phone for a bit. She even mentioned that she remembered Johnny and Mason talking about my mom before Johnny died. Her kindness in such an awkward situation was a gift I didn't expect but truly appreciated.

She mentioned that she and Johnny had one son together, Eric. She said she'd talk to him when the time felt right and explain my situation. If he was interested in connecting, she promised to pass along my name and number. I thanked her, and we said goodbye. As I hung up, I wasn't sure if I'd ever hear from them again. I hoped I would. I prayed I would. And honestly, I did a lot of praying in those days.

I was sitting at my young son's baseball game, perched on the hard metal bleachers at the top of the stands. The late afternoon sun hung lazily in the sky, casting a golden glow over the field. Dust from the infield rose in little puffs as the players shifted their feet, waiting for the next pitch. The rhythmic sounds of the game filled the air—the sharp crack of the bat, the thud of a ball smacking into a well-worn glove, the occasional metallic clank of a bat being tossed aside. Parents cheered, some calling out their kids' names, while younger siblings ran along the edge of the stands, their giggles mixing with the scent of freshly cut grass, buttery popcorn, and the sticky sweetness of melted snow cones.

I was half-listening, caught somewhere between watching my son on the field and the familiar hum of baseball that had become part of my life as a sports mom.

Then my phone buzzed.

I almost didn't check it. Maybe it was a reminder I'd set and forgotten about, or some spam call about my car's "extended warranty." But something—a nudge, a feeling deep in my gut—made me glance down.

A number I didn't recognize.

My stomach tightened.

For a second, I debated letting it go to voicemail. But as I looked back at my son, crouched in position, his small frame ready for the next play, I knew I had to answer.

I swiped to accept.

"Hello?"

For a moment, all I heard was breathing. Then— "Melissa?"

The voice was warm, excited, familiar in a way that didn't make sense. There was something in his tone—something buzzing just beneath the surface. "This is Eric."

My mind raced. **Eric?** I scrambled to place the name. And then it hit me.

The possibility. The hope. The reason my stomach had dropped the moment I saw that unknown number.

Eric—the man who might be my brother.

The baseball game faded into a distant hum, the laughter, the cheers, the thud of the ball all muffling as my world narrowed to this moment. The excitement in his voice matched mine. The words tumbled out quickly, both of us caught in the thrill of the unknown, the wild, almost impossible idea that life had just taken an unexpected turn. We talked. And talked. We spent hours on the phone, laughing, swapping memories, marveling at the sheer twists and turns life can take.

Eric shared stories about his dad, painting a picture of what life had been like growing up with him. I soaked up every detail, every word, trying to imagine a life that might have been mine. I could hear it in his voice—the unspoken wonder, the cautious hope, the nervous energy beneath the excitement.

Was this real? Could we really be siblings?

I hugged my free arm around my waist, grounding myself as I listened, as I let myself lean into the possibility. Because this wasn't just a phone call. It was a door opening. And on the other side? Maybe, just maybe, the family I had been searching for all along.

When the idea of a DNA test came up, Eric was all in. We compared schedules, I ordered the test, and soon enough, I was packing my bags for a road trip to Amarillo.

The time I spent there was a whirlwind. Eric and I pored over photo albums, swapped more stories, and got to know each other in a way that felt like we'd been doing it forever. Of course, we also swabbed our mouths for the all-important DNA test. I sent it off, and then the waiting began.

Was it really possible? Had I stumbled onto the answer to my search so quickly? Could it be this easy? What do you think? Of course not. But in that moment, the hope was alive, and I clung to it like a lifeline.

I waited impatiently for the results to come back. Brutal doesn't even begin to describe it. My mind wouldn't stop spinning—wondering if, by some miracle, I had stumbled onto the answer. Could it really be that easy? Had I just met my younger brother? Spent hours on the phone with my uncle? My thoughts were doing Olympic-level gymnastics, flipping between hope and doubt.

The day the email arrived; my stomach was in knots. Seeing the subject line from the DNA company, felt like time stood still. I sat at my computer, fingers hovering over the mouse, heart pounding. But deep down, I already knew. Even before I clicked, I felt it in my gut. I hadn't found my father. Eric wasn't my brother. Mason wasn't my uncle. This wasn't my family.

I was back at square one.

I even tried to find Mom's old roommate from Montana, but without a last name and no social media back then, I was out of luck. Time to get creative. I joined a Facebook group for people who had lived in or been stationed in Glasgow, Montana, hoping someone might remember Mom or Allen. I reached out to total strangers who were stationed there at the time I was conceived, just on the slim chance they'd know something. But nothing.

Six months into my search, I'd spoken to every family member I could think of, reached out to old friends, and messaged complete strangers in Facebook groups. Still, I was no closer to the answers I desperately wanted. I wasn't making progress, but I wasn't about to give up either. I had questions, and I needed answers. What I was—was frustrated. Stuck. Completely stuck.

I'm tenacious, though. Or maybe just plain stubborn—bloody stubborn, if I'm being honest. Since I'd hit a roadblock, I decided to shift gears for a bit. Ancestry has always been important to me, and for the longest time, I was so proud to say I was part Cherokee. Right now, I wish I could drop an emoji in here. Seriously—just look at me. Blonde hair, blue eyes, fair skin—I totally scream Native American, right? Insert a classic eye roll here, because even I had to admit that didn't quite add up.

It was one of the many little hints that Allen wasn't my biological father. And honestly? Losing that piece of identity was one of the saddest parts of this whole mess for me. No longer part Cherokee? That stung. So, what was I?

With my other leads drying up, I decided to try something new: DNA testing. It felt like a long shot, but at this point, I needed something—anything—to keep my search alive.

By this time, there were all kinds of DNA tests out there—ones to explore your ancestry, genetics, even your health. Naturally, I decided to try one. I went with Ancestry.com since I already had a membership and was working on my family tree. But you know what I didn't stop to think about when I ordered that kit? That I was about to get a bunch of family matches. Matches that could lead me straight to my father. So, I ordered the DNA kit, spit in the tube (gross, but necessary), and sent it off. That tiny little vial held the potential to completely reshape how I understood myself. Who I was. Where I came from. It was equal parts terrifying and exciting.

Then came the hard part: waiting. For weeks, I checked my email like it was a lifeline, hoping—praying—that the results would finally bring me closer to the answers I'd been searching for.

I waited anxiously for the results—results that might finally tell me more about my ancestors, about me. Who was I, really? What made me ... me? I knew I'd probably lose the claim to being Cherokee, but I couldn't have guessed what I'd gain. And when the email finally arrived, it was like striking gold—for the heritage at least.

Sitting in the study, at the computer, my hands trembled as I clicked on the email notification. The words "Your DNA Results Are In" glared back at me from the subject line. For weeks, I'd been waiting for this moment, clinging to the fragile hope that this would finally be it—the answers I'd been searching for, the missing piece of my identity. My breath quickened, and I could feel the drumbeat of my heart echoing in my ears.

The study was dimly lit, the soft glow of the computer screen casting shadows on the walls. The house was quiet, but my mind was anything but. What if this was it? What if I finally found him? What if the answers I needed were only a few clicks away? My fingers hovered over the mouse, shaky and hesitant, before I mustered the courage to click.

As the results loaded, the familiar logo of the DNA testing site filled the screen, followed by a cascade of names—second cousins. Distant relatives. Matches that felt like whispers of possibility. My eyes scanned the list, desperate for something—anything—that stood out. But there was nothing. No father. No siblings. Just names I didn't recognize, and connections too far removed to bring me closer to the truth.

My heart sank, the weight of disappointment settled heavily in my chest. I leaned back in my chair, the smooth leather cool against my back, its gentle creak breaking the stillness of the room. My mouth felt dry, my palms damp with sweat as I gripped the edge of the desk. Weeks of anticipation had built to this moment, and now it felt like the air had been knocked out of me.

I scrolled through the matches again, slower this time, hoping I'd missed something. But the list remained the same, each name like a closed door. The tears came suddenly, hot and stinging, blurring the screen in front of me. I brushed them away, frustrated with myself for crying, for letting the disappointment overwhelm me. But I couldn't help it. I'd pinned so much on this—on finally finding a name, a connection, a thread to pull that would lead me to the truth.

I closed my eyes, taking a deep breath, trying to steady myself. This wasn't the end, I told myself. It was just another step, another piece of the puzzle. But at that moment, it didn't feel like progress. It felt like I was further from the truth than ever.

The silence of the room seemed deafening now; the hum of the computer is the only sound. I looked at the screen, at the names that didn't hold the answers I'd hoped for, and let the disappointment wash over me. I didn't know what to do next, but I knew one thing for certain: I couldn't give up. Not yet. Not when the truth was still out there, waiting to be found.

It turns out my roots were planted in places I'd always dreamed of visiting: England, Scotland, Wales, and Ireland. The rolling green hills, ancient castles, and rich histories I'd read about as a child suddenly felt like pieces of my own story. A little touch of Norway and Sweden gave me visions of fearless Vikings sailing across stormy seas. And a sprinkling of Cameroon, Congo, and Western Bantu added a vibrant, unexpected layer to my identity. My heritage was richer, more diverse, and more fascinating than I could have imagined. For the first time in a long while, I felt a spark of connection—not just to my past, but to something bigger than myself.

And then there were the names. My screen lit up with names I'd never seen before—names that didn't belong to the family I'd grown up with but were somehow connected to me. My heart raced; my breath caught in my throat as I stared at those unfamiliar names. Could one of these people hold the key to finding my father?

The possibility sent a rush of adrenaline through me, making my hands shake as I hovered over each name. My stomach churned with a mixture of excitement and nerves. I clicked through the matches, my eyes scanning for clues, each name a tiny thread in the tapestry of my story. Some were close matches, others distant, but they all represented a connection—a bridge to the truth I'd been chasing for so long. The hum of the computer filled the quiet room as I leaned closer to the screen, my fingers trembling over the keyboard. With every click, I felt a jolt of hope. My heart pounded as I scrolled through the list, trying to piece together how each name fit into my puzzle. The names were just the beginning, but they felt like an open door—a glimmer of light breaking through the fog of uncertainty.

For years, I'd felt like a branch without a tree, disconnected and adrift. But now, with each new name, I began to see the outline of something I'd longed for: belonging. These people, these strangers, were somehow part of me, and I couldn't wait to find out how.

Was it easy? Of course not. When does life ever give you the easy path? And if it did, would we even appreciate it? Probably not. I had plenty of cousin matches. But no siblings. No paternal. Because, naturally, that would've been too easy. My closest matches were a couple of second cousins, but we couldn't connect the dots.

So, I decided to cast my net a little wider and tested with 23andMe. The results? More of the same. Lots of cousins. No first cousins. No siblings. No direct paternal matches. It felt like I was assembling a puzzle with half the pieces missing—or worse, trying to make sense of a map without knowing where it even began.

For months, I emailed strangers—cousins and distant relatives who popped up on my DNA matches. I poured my heart out, shared my story, and asked countless questions, hoping someone, anyone, might hold the missing piece. A few tried to help, doing their best to piece together the fragments, but nothing clicked. For multiple reasons, the trail kept running cold. Frustration settled in, and I could feel the weight of defeat creeping closer.

With my DNA results only taking me so far, I decided it was time to call in the professionals. A quick email to Ancestry's team laid everything out—what I'd done, where I'd searched, and how desperate I was for answers. That's when a professional genealogist stepped in, and suddenly, the search had a fresh burst of energy.

He emailed me back and set up a time for a call. From the moment we started talking, he was kind and encouraging, assuring me that I wasn't as "hopeless" of a case as I had feared. His words were a balm for my frazzled nerves. He praised the groundwork I'd already done, saying I'd completed much of what they'd typically recommend. Then he asked a few clarifying questions—and laid out the plan: at most, it should take six months to find my answer.

The cost? Reasonable. The timeline? Logical. The hope? Rekindled.

They kept me updated throughout the process, occasionally reaching out with a question or to confirm a new lead they'd uncovered. Each email or phone call felt like a small nudge of reassurance—a reminder that the search was in good hands. For the first time in a long time, I felt a bit of relief.

Through it all, Chuck Rod, my sweet husband, stood steady beside me. He was never intimidated by my search for my birth father. He didn't flinch at the ache I still carried. He just stayed— strong, faithful, and quiet in the way only the best kind of men are. He didn't compete with my past. He redeemed it.

When leads went cold and the waiting got heavy, I turned to prayer. I'd been praying from the beginning, but now my prayers carried a different edge—anticipation. A sense that this long chapter of my life was finally nearing its conclusion. I could almost see the light at the end of the tunnel, and the thought of finally having answers filled me with cautious joy.

And then—just as the finish line came into view—they hit a snag.

Just when I thought the finish line was finally in sight, the genealogist called with news I didn't see coming—another delay. My heart sank. The tunnel that once seemed so short suddenly stretched out again, endless and dim. But giving up? That wasn't even on the table. Not when I'd come this far, not when I was so close.

During the call, he apologized, explaining that despite their earlier confidence that the search would take no more than six months, they still hadn't cracked the case. He asked if I was willing to give them another month to keep digging. Was I? Of course! How could I stop now? The thought of quitting so close to the answers I'd been chasing for a lifetime wasn't even an option. "Keep going," I told him. "I'll wait."

While Ancestry.com was hard at work, I kept busy in my own way—praying and digging wherever I could. Every time I hit a dead end, I turned to prayer, asking for patience, guidance, and the wisdom to see what God had in store. This wasn't just about finding my father anymore. It had become about something bigger—about trusting that God's timing would bring the answers exactly when I was ready to receive them.

He and his team remained confident. "We're close," they assured me. And I could feel it—so close I could almost taste it. A name, a face, a connection to the missing piece of my life was within reach. I tried to keep calm, to quiet the whirlwind of emotions in my heart, but my mind wouldn't stop racing. What would it be like to finally know? To have answers to the questions that had haunted me for so long?

Days turned into weeks, and every passing moment felt like an eternity. Just as the frustration started to creep back in, God stepped in with a twist I never saw coming—a gift I couldn't have dreamed up. The answers I'd been waiting for were right around the corner, but they were coming in a way I never anticipated.

Field Notes:
Evidence for Healing

Earthly DNA may reveal facts, but divine DNA defines truth.

REFLECTION QUESTIONS

- Have you ever had to wait for something that felt deeply personal?

- What helped you hold on when the answers were delayed?

- How do you balance trusting God and taking action?

ENCOURAGEMENT

Sometimes, healing takes research. Sometimes, it takes waiting. And sometimes, it takes mailing a vial of spit and trusting God to use it. Even in the unknown, God is ahead of you—lining up answers, preparing your heart, and making sure the right doors open at the right time.

WRITING PROMPT

Write about a time when waiting stretched you. What were you hoping for? What emotions did the waiting stir up? And what did you discover—about God, about yourself, or about what truly matters?

SCRIPTURE ANCHOR

"Yet to all who did receive him, to those who believed in his name, he gave the right to become children of God—" – **John 1:12**

PRAYER

Lord, thank You for walking with me through the waiting, through the wondering, and through every unanswered question. Help me to trust that You are still working, even when the path feels uncertain. Give me strength to keep hoping, courage to keep praying, and faith to believe that Your timing is always good. Amen.

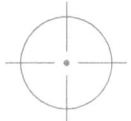

When Heaven Opened: Meeting My Father Through God's Grace

"And afterward, I will pour out my Spirit on all people. Your sons and daughters will prophesy, your old men will dream dreams, your young men will see visions."
– Joel 2:28

"'If You can?' said Jesus, 'Everything is possible for him who believes.'"
– Mark 9:23

This moment needed its own chapter because, for me, it's the heart of everything. God gave me a miraculous, deeply personal gift—one that, no matter what anyone else might think, I know was real! I didn't want this to get buried in everything else because, to me, it deserves the spotlight. It was only because of God that I had this incredible moment, one that brought me peace and felt like a reminder that He was with me every step of the way.

I had given the okay for Ancestry.com to continue the search. They believed they were close to an answer for me. Time was ticking away. From the very beginning, one of my concerns was that whoever my father was, he might already be dead. Considering I was born during the Vietnam War, it seemed possible that my father had been deployed and never returned. For all I knew, he had been sent away at some point and never made it back home. Since I knew Mom was near an Air Force base when I was conceived, I strongly suspected my father was in the Air Force—and I was right, though it took time to confirm.

As I said, the folks at Ancestry.com were amazing. They worked diligently on my mystery, helping me find the man who was my biological father. They had a couple of people working on it, and I received multiple emails and phone calls—with questions to clarify things as well as to update me on the latest news and progress.

Then came the call—they were almost there but still needed a little more time. And I gave them the time they were requesting. How could I not?

There was no way I was willing to stop now. I was so close to the answers I needed—craved even. Through this whole journey, as I stumbled along, I prayed. I cried. I begged. I pleaded. I yelled. I waited, though impatiently at times.

I'd already gone down this path, why did I have to do it again?! *GOD!! WHY??* Why me? Why again? I'd already lived through this hurt and pain. The feelings of being abandoned, of feeling unloved. Why did I have to go through it all over again?

But I wasn't—not really. At least, not fully the same. This time, I knew that God was there. That He loved me and wanted the best for me. I knew that, even during the pain and sorrow, He held me close and loved me. He was there the first time, but remember—I was a self-involved teen, only thinking of myself and unable to see past the end of my nose.

I knew it would be okay. No matter what. Even if I never found the man who was my biological father. Because God knew. God knew who he was. God knew where he was. And God knew how much I needed to know.

I was praying, begging God to let me meet him. I cried. I pleaded. And then I said, "But only if it's what You want. Only if it's what's best. But please." I gave it to God. That night, before bed, I thanked Him. For always being there. For always loving me. For being my Daddy. The Father who never left, never disappointed, and always wanted the best for me. And then, I went to sleep.

The next morning, I woke up so happy. At peace. Because I'd had the loveliest dream.

I was in a small white room, like a waiting room. When I say small, I mean *small*. There were four white chairs, facing each other. No other furniture. Four white walls, no doors, no windows. And when I say white, I mean *bright* white. Yet the room was empty and somehow comforting, as if it was created just for us. The light was bright but warm, almost heavenly. I was sitting in one of the chairs, and across from me sat two men. One was young, late teens or maybe early twenties. He had a buzz cut, and he made me think of the military, even though he wore jeans and a short-sleeve button-down shirt. The other man was older, maybe in his forties, with a beard and mustache. The three of us were talking. They were both smiling. Then, after a while, the younger man—sitting on the left side of the older one—with his right hand, punched the other man in the arm and said: "Dude! She's your daughter!" The man with the facial hair grinned even bigger, nodded his head, and replied: "Yes, yes, she is." At that moment, we all stood up. They both hugged me. The younger man was giddy, bouncing on the balls of his feet, with a huge grin on his face. He kept repeating: "Dude, she's your daughter!" We talked for some time, and they mentioned how I looked like their sister—or maybe my sister? I wasn't clear on that part. We hugged again. They told me they loved me. They said how excited they were to meet me. As we hugged one last time, they said they would be seeing me and that they loved me.

And then I woke up. It felt so real. More vivid than any dream I have ever had. For the first time in this journey, I felt an overwhelming sense of peace, as if God Himself had orchestrated that meeting. I couldn't stop smiling. It was a wonderful feeling upon waking. The peace and joy I felt were indescribable. I knew that God was in control. And that no matter what, one day, I would know who my father was.

Two weeks later, I received an email from Ancestry.com—the report on their findings.

The pro genealogist had determined, through my DNA and others, that my father was one of two brothers, but they were not willing to state definitively which one. Neither man had any known children, and both were deceased. Their names were Danny and

David Demings. They did, however, have a sister still living in Texas—in the Dallas area. Just three hours from me. For practical reasons and the process of elimination, it was fairly easy to determine which brother was my father.

David Demings died on May 12, 1969, in Binh, Long Xuyen, An Giang, Vietnam at the age of 19. Danny Demings died in Texas on October 8, 2005, at the age of 58. Now, remember—I was conceived in Glasgow, Montana, in January 1968. Danny was in the Air Force, stationed in Glasgow at the time. David, on the other hand, was still in high school, preparing to graduate and join the Army. Can you guess who my biological father is? Let me go out on a limb here and say ... that would be Danny.

With this revelation, I reached out to their sister, Elaine. From the very start, Elaine was amazing. Just imagine—walking to your mailbox on a late summer day, expecting nothing more than bills and junk mail, only to find a letter that changes your world. That's exactly what happened to her. It was a day like any other—warm and quiet—as Elaine made her usual walk to retrieve the mail. She wasn't expecting anything special. But there it was—a large manila envelope with unfamiliar handwriting, a stranger's name, and an address she didn't recognize.

I can only imagine what must have gone through her mind as she stood there, letter in hand, reading words that would change everything. Shock. Confusion. Maybe even disbelief. A daughter? A niece? A cousin—after 45 years? How do you process something like that?

I made copies of the report and wrote a letter explaining who I was and who I believed my biological father was. I tried my best to reassure this stranger that I wasn't after anything—although, if I were being completely honest, that wasn't the whole truth.

I *did* want something. I wanted to know: What did Danny look like? What kind of man was he? What were their parents—my grandparents—like? Did I look like him? Did I have any characteristics from him?

I wanted information. Anything and everything she was willing to share with me. And share she did!

In my packet, I included my cell phone number, my landline number (yes, we still had one at that point!), my email, and my physical address. Basically, any and every possible way she could reach me. I was a nervous wreck when I sent that packet off. What would she think? Would she think it was a scam? Would she believe I was a con artist? Would she throw it in the trash without even looking at it? Would she call or write me? Would I ever hear from her?

I was scared—terrified, really—that I was going to be cast aside again. That, once again, my father's family wouldn't want me.

But I didn't have to wait long for a response. I received a call. When the phone rang, my heart raced. I answered, and on the other end was Elaine's voice—calm, steady, but with a warmth that immediately put me at ease. I had no idea what to expect. Would she be hesitant? Skeptical? Upset? But instead, she greeted me with a kindness that melted away any anxiety I had. Her words were filled with genuine curiosity and a surprising openness. From that very first conversation, it felt like we were meant to connect, and every call since has been just as welcoming and kind.

At that moment, I began to realize how incredibly fortunate I was. Elaine's openness was more than I could have hoped for—

it was a gift. She didn't have to welcome me. She didn't have to embrace the idea of a newfound niece. But she did. And in that, I found the family I had long been searching for. Whatever her initial reaction was, when she called me, it was nothing short of warmth and kindness. She never doubted me. She never questioned if I was trying to string her along with some wild tale. Instead, she welcomed me with open arms and an open heart.

Elaine was firm in her acceptance of me, but she was also thoughtful about my journey in finding Danny. She didn't want me to ever question if he was truly my father or not. So, she encouraged me to take a DNA test with her, ensuring I would never doubt my place in the family. Without hesitation, I ordered the test and took it with me when I went to visit her in person.

Before my trip, I gathered a wide variety of pictures—from birth to that very day. I made copies to take with me and give to her. Turns out, she had the same idea. Elaine had gathered pictures of her brothers, her parents, and other extended family members. She made copies of them for me. Two people, connected by blood, now connecting through memories and history, exchanging pieces of the past to bridge the gap of time.

When I arrived at Elaine's house and saw her for the first time, I realized something astonishing—I looked like her. We sat at the kitchen table, talking and flipping through our respective photos. As we reminisced, I shared with her the dream I had—the one where I met two men I had never seen before but somehow knew. At this point, I hadn't yet seen pictures of Danny or David. But when I described the young man in my dream, Elaine suddenly dug through the photos and pulled out one of David. It was him—the young man from my dream.

Next, she pulled out pictures of Danny. Most of them showed him with a mustache, but a few were clean-shaven. I studied them and admitted, *"I can kind of see a resemblance to the other man in my dream."* At first, Elaine dismissed it. *"Danny never had a beard,"* she said.

Then suddenly— "Wait!" She jumped up and hurried off, quickly returning with a photo in her hand. It was Danny. With a beard. It was him—the man from my dream.

Looking through those photos, it became clear—God had given me more than answers—He had given me peace. His love extended beyond time and reality, allowing me a glimpse of something precious. I may not have had the chance to meet my father in life, but through God's grace, I was given a gift far beyond what I ever imagined. Through His love, God let me meet these two men. I may not have known them in life, but He opened the gates of Heaven— just for a brief visit. To bring me peace and belonging in a way I'd never dreamed. He gave me a gift I hadn't even known I needed—a gift of love.

Field Notes:
Evidence for Healing

Sometimes God reveals the truth not through evidence, but through encounters with HIM.

REFLECTION QUESTIONS

- Have you ever received a dream, impression, or insight that felt like it came straight from God?

- How do you respond when God speaks to you in ways you weren't expecting?

- What dreams—literal or metaphorical—have brought you closer to understanding your identity?

ENCOURAGEMENT

God doesn't always speak through thunder and fire. Sometimes, He shows up in the quiet, the intimate, the in-between. Don't discount the supernatural just because it doesn't look like what you expected. He knows how to reach your heart.

WRITING PROMPT

Write about a dream or moment of clarity that shifted something in you. What did it reveal? What did it prepare you for?

SCRIPTURE ANCHOR

"Call to me and I will answer you and tell you great and unsearchable things you do not know."

– Jeremiah 33:3

PRAYER

Lord, You are the God who speaks in whispers and wonders. Tune my heart to recognize Your voice in the quiet and the chaos. When answers seem distant, anchor me in Your peace. When clarity feels just out of reach, remind me that You are never far. I invite You to speak to me in ways my soul will understand—and I will wait, trusting that Your timing and Your truth are always perfect. Amen.

The Family I Found: A Journey of Discovery & Acceptance

"He has made everything beautiful in its time. He has also set eternity in the human heart; yet no one can fathom what God has done from beginning to end."
— **Ecclesiastes 3:11**

Finding my father was my focus, but God wasn't just working on my family tree—

He was reshaping my heart. I had always felt the ache of something missing, but I didn't realize He was preparing to fill those empty spaces with more love, grace, and family than I'd ever dreamed possible.

I was always so obsessed with finding my father—knowing who he was. Knowing who I was.

It never really occurred to me that with him would come a whole family. Sure, I was curious about siblings, grandparents, aunts, and uncles, but I didn't give it much thought beyond that.

My focus was laser-sharp: find him. But while I was fixated on the search, God had a much bigger picture in mind.

When I was searching, I couldn't have imagined what lay ahead. I didn't know that I wouldn't get to meet my father here on earth. That I would just barely miss the chance to meet my Grandma Babe. That my grandfather had passed long before. That my Uncle David Demings had died when I was just a few months old. I didn't realize all the things I would miss out on.

But even more, I couldn't have dreamed of the incredible family I had out there waiting for me to find them.

When I got the DNA results and reached out to my Aunt Elaine, I was welcomed with open arms—no questions. No hesitation. It was an incredible feeling—one I'll never forget.

Discovering who my father was felt like a dream come true, but being embraced so completely by his family? That was beyond anything I could have ever hoped for. I spent so much of my life searching for Allen—trying to build something real with him. It felt like such a waste: all the hurt, pain, sorrow, and anger. What was it all for? Thinking about him. Part of me still says it was a waste, but was it really? I wouldn't be who I am if I hadn't walked the path I did to get to where I am. If I hadn't gone through the hard times in my life that I did, I wouldn't have relied on God. I wouldn't have called out to Him. I wouldn't be the woman of God that I am today.

I grieved Allen's death—not just the man, but the father figure I longed for but never truly had. All the missed opportunities weighed on me, but then I learned the truth: he wasn't my father after all. It was never his responsibility to be there.

Yes, it was funny at first finding out that Allen wasn't my birth father. Eventually, though, it hurt. I spent ten years building a relationship with him before he passed, and then fourteen more mourning what could have been. Discovering Allen wasn't my birth father added another layer of loss. It was like losing him all over again—this time, for good.

No matter how badly our relationship may have gone, no matter how frustrated I was at times, no matter what jokes I would crack ... the bottom line was I had believed he was my father, and he loved me in his way, and he did the best he could do. He tried to protect me in his way. And there I was, losing him once again.

I figured this was the final time. I didn't believe there was any other way for me to lose him.

I did love him, and it hurt saying goodbye ... again.

When I finally found my birth father and his family, I planned a trip to the area of Oklahoma where they were from. But before heading there, I took a detour to the southeastern corner of the state. I drove to Heavener, Oklahoma, one last time.

I wanted to see Lola's house, to drive past it and see if it was still standing.

It was.

Then, I went to the cemetery. I've never been one to visit cemeteries often, but this time, I felt a pull—a quiet, insistent nudge that I couldn't ignore. It wasn't about the headstone or the physical place. It was about her. Somehow, standing there felt like the closest I could get to sitting at Lola's kitchen table again, hearing her warm laughter, and watching her hands move gracefully as she shared stories or prayed over me.

The air was crisp, the kind that makes you wrap your arms around yourself for warmth. The sky was a pale shade of blue, dotted with soft, lazy clouds. The ground beneath my feet was uneven, and I could hear the crunch of fallen leaves as I walked. When I reached her grave, I stood there for a moment, letting the stillness settle over me. The world seemed quieter there, as though even nature wanted to honor her memory.

I knelt, brushing some stray leaves away from the headstone, and smiled faintly at the sight of her name etched into the granite. It felt strange, seeing it there, so final. But then, I remembered the woman who had always been larger than life to me—the one whose presence couldn't be confined to a name on a stone.

"I wanted to say thank you," I whispered, my voice barely audible in the stillness. "Thank you for welcoming me into the family, for loving me without hesitation, for making me feel like I belonged."

I could almost hear her voice in my mind, gentle and frail, telling me how much she loved me, how proud she was of me. My heart ached, but it also swelled with gratitude. "You didn't have to love me, you know," I continued, my voice cracking. "But you did. From the moment we met, you made me feel like I mattered—like I was wanted—and safe."

The wind picked up slightly, rustling the leaves around me, and for a moment, I let myself imagine it was her way of responding, her spirit reminding me that love doesn't end—it just changes form.

"I hope I made you proud," I said, tears streaming down my cheeks now. "I hope you know how much you meant to me, how much your love carried me through some of the hardest times in my life. You taught me about faith, about strength, about the kind of love that doesn't waver."

As I stood there, I felt the weight of everything I hadn't said, everything I wished I could have told her when she was alive. I told her about my journey, about the truths I'd uncovered and the family I'd found. I told her how much I missed her, how I still missed the way her Bible seemed to hold all the answers, how I missed the comfort of her kitchen and the way her prayers could calm even the most restless heart.

"Thank you for showing me God's love," I said finally, my voice trembling. "Thank you for being the grandmother I didn't even know I needed. You were such a gift, Lola. And I hope you know that."

The wind seemed to wrap around me then, a gentle embrace that made me feel like, somehow, she did know. And as I stood there, letting the moment wash over me, I felt a sense of peace I hadn't expected. It wasn't goodbye—not really. It was just another way of saying, "I love you," and trusting that love would carry us both.

As I turned to leave, I felt lighter. Not because the grief was gone, but because I knew that the love Lola had given me would stay with me forever, woven into the fabric of who I was. And for that, I would always be grateful.

I sat there with Allen too, whispering into the silence. The weight of everything—years of questions, disappointments, and hurt—seemed to press against my chest. But in that moment, it felt like the silence was listening, like the air itself held space for the words I needed to say.

"I'm sorry," I whispered. Sorry for the things I'd said in anger, for the moments when my hurt had spoken louder than my love. Sorry for not understanding him better, for not seeing him as the flawed, complicated man he was until it was too late. Sorry for expecting him to be someone he wasn't capable of being.

"I love you," I said, my voice trembling. It wasn't an easy love—it was a love wrapped in layers of pain and confusion, but it was love all the same. Despite everything, I had loved him, and I needed him to know that.

"I forgive you," I said, the words catching in my throat as they left my lips. I forgave him for the rejection, for the promises he didn't keep, for the years of wondering if I was somehow unworthy. And in that forgiveness, I felt the weight of his absence begin to lift. The burden I had carried for so long—the anger, the resentment, the sadness—finally began to loosen its grip on my heart.

As I stood at Allen's grave, I realized that forgiveness wasn't about excusing his absence or justifying his choices—it was about releasing the pain they caused. Forgiveness didn't mean pretending the hurt hadn't happened or erasing the years of disappointment. It meant choosing not to let that pain define me anymore. It meant letting go of the bitterness that had quietly taken root in my heart.

In that quiet moment, I felt the weight of all the years I'd carried the anger, the sadness, and the questions. I thought of how many times God had forgiven me—how often He had looked past my failings, my stubbornness, and my doubts, and had chosen love instead. That same grace He had poured out for me was the grace I now wanted to extend to Allen.

"I forgive you," I whispered, the words catching in my throat. "Not because you earned it, but because I can't carry this anymore."

Tears fell freely as I released years of pain and anger, leaving them there at the grave, where they could no longer hold me captive. In that act of forgiveness, I felt a strange, unexpected peace. It wasn't just about Allen anymore—it was about me. It was about letting God heal the places I had kept hidden, the ones I hadn't even realized still needed mending.

Then came the question I'd been circling around since the moment I realized I hadn't known the whole story. "Did you know?" I asked, my voice barely more than a whisper. "Did you know I wasn't your daughter? Is that why you stayed away?" The words hung in the air, heavy and raw. I knew I'd never get an answer but saying them out loud gave me a strange sense of closure. For the first time, the question no longer felt like a wound—it was just part of the story, a thread in the tangled fabric of my life.

I sat there for a while, letting the silence stretch between us, feeling the warmth of the sun on my face and the coolness of the breeze on my skin. And then, with a deep breath, I said the words I hadn't realized I'd been holding back for so long: "Goodbye."

At that moment, something shifted. Saying goodbye wasn't just letting go of Allen—it was letting go of the hurt, the anger, the longing for him to be someone he couldn't be. It was accepting him as he was, flaws and all, and releasing the weight of expecting anything more. It was forgiving him for the times he let me down and forgiving myself for holding onto that hurt for so long.

I finally understood that he probably knew the truth all along—that I wasn't his daughter. Maybe that knowledge had shaped his distance, his hesitation to stay in my life. Or maybe it hadn't. Either way, I realized it didn't matter anymore. I couldn't change the past, and I couldn't keep carrying it with me.

Walking away that day, I felt lighter, freer, as though the chains of resentment and hurt had finally been broken. I didn't have all the answers, and I probably never would. But for the first time, that was okay. Forgiveness had allowed me to move forward, not with the burden of what was lost, but with the hope of what could be. And for that, I was grateful.

The love I had for Allen wasn't perfect, but it was real, and that was enough. The goodbye wasn't just for him—it was for me, too. It was a step toward healing, a way of saying, "I'm ready to move forward now." And as I walked away, I felt a quiet peace settle over me, as if God Himself was whispering, "It's time."

And with that, I drove away—for the last time.

As I drove away from Allen's grave, I felt a strange mix of emotions: relief, sadness, and a quiet, undeniable peace. Saying goodbye had been necessary, a final release of the weight I had carried for so long. But as one chapter closed, another was waiting to be written.

It was time to turn my heart and my journey toward the man I had been searching for all along—Danny.

How Danny became my father is one of those mysteries only God could write—one even the most seasoned investigator would struggle to crack. The facts were fuzzy, the timeline never quite made sense, and even the witnesses couldn't agree on the details. But I've learned that some case files aren't meant to be solved with logic—they're meant to be surrendered. And in His infinite wisdom, God stamped this one "Handled." He didn't need the story to be neat or the evidence to line up. Somehow—through His mercy, His timing, and His perfect plan—Danny became mine. Not by chance, not by DNA, but by divine design.

And honestly? That's the only explanation I need.

My destination was Holdenville, Oklahoma—the town where Danny had grown up, gone to school, and built the life I had never known. I wanted to see the places that had shaped him, to walk the same streets he once did, and to connect with the roots that had always been mine, even if I hadn't known it.

With every mile that passed, I felt a shift within me. For so long, my search had been tangled in uncertainty, in the ache of not knowing where I truly belonged. But now, with answers in hand and a new family waiting, I was ready to step into this next part of the story.

This journey wasn't just about visiting locations—it was about stepping into the past, discovering the pieces of Danny's life, and finding my place in the story that had been unfolding long before I ever knew to look for it.

Would you like to hear how wonderful Danny's family is? When Elaine welcomed me, it was like stepping into a warm embrace—one I didn't realize I'd been waiting for my whole life. Holdenville wasn't just a place; it was a piece of my father's heart. The small town had a quiet charm, with streets that seemed to echo stories from decades past. Elaine introduced me to her children and their families, making the experience even more emotional and exciting. Walking through the places tied to my father's life—the school he attended, the church where he was baptized, and even the cemetery where he is buried—felt like I was piecing together a part of myself that had been missing. Standing there, surrounded by fragments of his story, made everything feel so real—like I was finally connecting with the father I had longed to know.

I had the incredible privilege of meeting my great-aunt, Betty Ree. Sitting with Betty Ree was like stepping into a time machine. I only got to spend time with her in person once, but those few hours were unforgettable. Her stories weren't just tales—they were vivid tapestries of Danny's life, woven with laughter and tears.

She described his quirks with such affection that I could almost hear his laugh, see his smile. She painted such vivid pictures of my father, Danny, and other family members who were long gone, that it felt like they were right there in the room with us—sitting, talking, and laughing. It felt like she was introducing me to him.

Unfortunately, before I had the chance to meet more of the family, Betty Ree passed away. Even though I hadn't met many of the family members yet, I felt strongly about attending her funeral to say goodbye.

I met my Aunt Elaine and my cousin Angie at the church where her service was to be held. The plan was simple—stay under the radar. No big introductions, no dramatic revelations. I wouldn't be introduced as Danny's daughter or even as family. Just someone who had met and admired Betty Ree. Nothing more. Nothing less.

But that plan didn't last long. Angie and I were standing off to the side, chatting quietly, when a woman walked up to us. I assumed she must know Angie, but instead, she turned to me and said— "You are Danny's daughter."

It wasn't a question. It was a statement—a fact. She knew.

I'd gone to Betty Ree's funeral hoping to quietly pay my respects, but God had other plans. The moment that woman walked up to me and said, "You're Danny's daughter," it felt like a door swung open.

Suddenly, I wasn't an outsider anymore—I was family.

The hugs, the smiles, the tears of recognition made me realize that God had been working behind the scenes all along, preparing their hearts just as He'd prepared mine.

From that moment, everything changed. Before I knew it, I had met most of the family. After the service, we spent more time together, and almost everyone I spoke with commented on how much I looked like Danny or Elaine, how I had Danny's mannerisms and how my speech patterns resembled his. They welcomed me with open arms, and by the end of the day, plans were already in motion for a "Cousin Reunion," so we could all spend more time together and really get to know one another. It was a whirlwind of unexpected emotions. Overwhelming. But above all—it was heartwarming.

But wait—there's more! Turns out, Danny was married at the time of his death, and he had two stepdaughters. They live out in Las Vegas, Nevada, with my stepmother, who's originally from Thailand. When I finally reached out, I was met with open arms and another warm welcome! (seriously, God is good!). I've even made the trek out west to meet these incredible ladies in person, along with my new aunties. Reaching out to Danny's wife and stepdaughters was nerve-wracking. What if they didn't want to hear from me? But their kindness melted my fears away.

Meeting them in Las Vegas felt surreal—I was stepping into yet another branch of my family tree, and they welcomed me as if I'd always been part of it. We laughed, shared stories, and built connections that felt as natural as breathing.

And here's another surprise—I have a younger half-sister in Thailand!

I've seen photos of her from when she was younger, but sadly, the family lost touch with her after Danny passed. I'm praying she comes back into their lives one day—maybe even mine—but I know that's in God's hands.

Knowing I have a sister out there, across an ocean, is both thrilling and bittersweet. I've seen her photos and wondered—does she know she has a sibling waiting to meet her? I pray for her often, trusting that God's timing will bring us together one day. Until then, she's a part of the story I hold close to my heart.

With all these new family connections, I've learned so much about Danny—the funny quirks and habits that made him so special and unique. And here's the kicker: My sons and I have unknowingly inherited some of those same idiosyncrasies. The little things that made him, him, are now pieces of us too. It's like God quietly tied a thread from Danny to this beautiful, blended family—one that stretches across states and continents—and I couldn't feel more grateful to be part of it.

Danny's legacy is woven into the fabric of my family in ways that both surprise and delight me. Through stories and memories shared by those who knew him, I've come to see how his quirks and personality traits live on in my sons and me.

One of the most endearing parts of his character was his knack for mimicking accents. Whether it was a thick Southern drawl, a posh British lilt, or something in between, Danny could bring it to life with uncanny accuracy. It's a trait that makes its way into my boys' playful conversations and brings a smile to my face every time.

His unique humor and ability to find lightness in the smallest things are gifts I now see reflected in our family.

It's as if Danny's legacy whispers through us, connecting the dots between who he was and who we are. And while he's no longer here, those echoes of his laughter, charm, and wit remind me that his presence will always be felt.

Looking back, I see how God has woven a masterpiece out of my search.

The family I found isn't perfect—no family is—but they are mine. And in every laugh, every story, every moment of connection, I feel God's love reminding me that He has always known the plan, even when I didn't.

Family is a gift, and finding mine has shown me that God's gifts are always better than anything I could have imagined.

I began this journey searching for one man, but God gave me so much more. He gave me stories, faces, connections, and a family that spans generations and continents. He gave me pieces of my father, but He also gave me pieces of Himself—grace, love, and belonging. For that, I will always be thankful.

Field Notes:
Evidence for Healing

Family isn't always who shares your blood; it's who shares your heart.

REFLECTION QUESTIONS

- Have you ever found yourself embraced in a way that healed old wounds?

- What does "family" mean to you now—biological or chosen?

- How do you receive love when it shows up unexpectedly?

WRITING PROMPT

Write about a moment when you felt truly seen and welcomed. What made that moment healing?

ENCOURAGEMENT

Sometimes the family God has for us comes from the most unexpected places. You may not even know you're missing them until they show up—and when they do, healing comes with them.

SCRIPTURE ANCHOR

"Whoever does God's will is my brother and sister and mother."

– Mark 3:35

PRAYER

Father God, thank You for the gift of family—whether by birth, by choice, or by miracle. Thank You for weaving people into my story exactly when I needed them. Help me to see the beauty in the connections You've made, even when the path to them wasn't easy. Teach me to cherish those You've brought into my life, and remind me that in You, I am always fully known, fully seen, and fully loved. Amen.

My Abba Father: Forgiveness, Grace, & Unwavering Love

"Be kind and compassionate to one another, forgiving each other,
just as in Christ God forgave you."
– Ephesians 4:32

G od is a good Father.

He loves us deeply, even when His answers come in ways we don't expect. Through my journey, He showed me that faith, patience, and forgiveness are not just lessons but gifts that transform us.

Yet, we should be mindful of what we ask for, as He often gives us what we need rather than what we envision—and rarely the easy way. But in every step, He teaches us, strengthens us, and walks with us, shaping us along our unique paths.

As I've said before, I wish I'd kept a journal back then. It might make it easier to remember every moment and feeling as I write. But instead, I ask God to bring back only what's important—what will help others see His work. I don't need to relive the pain to know how He's carried me through it. Instead, I trust Him to help me share the healing, the forgiveness, and the growth that came from my journey.

I do want to remember the joy. This might sound bizarre, but as horrible as it was, there were also some amazing times. For instance, even though I suddenly didn't have Lola as my great-grandmother, and I was no longer a part of the Cherokee Nation, I suddenly had an aunt and cousins who welcomed me with open arms. I had always admired the Irish and Scots and their struggles. Okay, so I may have said this before—but I always secretly hoped I had a little Scottish or Irish in me. And wouldn't you know it? My ancestors came through. Bagpipes and shamrocks, y'all. It's official.

One thing I prayed through it all … *Thy will be done.* Through all the pain. Through all the hurt. God is good. I kept reminding myself of that: He is God. He hears me. His plans are for me. He sees me. He has amazing things in store for me. I know He heard me. I was very vocal in my cries to Him. I made a point of reminding Him of His promises to me. His Word has a lot of promises in it, and I didn't hesitate to remind Him. I was like a small child begging and pestering their parent to do something. At times, I would stand in my house and cry, stomping my foot like a petulant two-year-old wanting her way.

I was hurting, and I wanted Him to fix it ... and fix it NOW. But He did it in His timing, with love. He never forgot His promises to me. He fulfilled them and more. I'm the one who will forget my promises to Him. I am a child of God. And like a child, sometimes I blow it. But no matter what, He is there. Watching me. Loving me. He looks at us like we do our own children at times—with love, forgiveness, understanding. Waiting for His children to come back and listen, to realize that He loves them no matter how they may mess up. No matter where they go, or what they do, He will love them and forgive them.

Such a simple prayer with a wealth of trust. Trust that it will be all we can hope for and more. So much more.

We really don't know what God sees that is coming. Whether it's good or bad, what twists and turns will occur, how we will react—He sees it all.

He sees the full picture, from beginning to end. Some days, I wish I could see the full picture—but would I really want to?

If I had known some of what I know now years ago, I would have made different choices—and in the process, I would have lost out on some of the joys of my life.

Your story begins long before you.

It encompasses so many people and the choices they make to get to the point of your conception and birth. Some choices are easy, some hard. Some are good, and some are bad.

But choices—no matter what they are—are always ours to make.

With God standing there, wanting us to choose Him and the path He knows is best for us.

God is so many things to us. But right now, I'm going to focus on the Father in Him.

Our Heavenly Father.

My whole life, I was looking for a father—one who was there the whole time. I just couldn't see Him. Not physically, and not always with my heart. But He was there. Holding me close the whole time. Loving me. Grieving with me. And telling me that He was there—if I'd just looked.

God is the ultimate Father. He sent His Son, Jesus, to Earth, far away from His home—for me. He sent my Big Brother down here to make sure that one day, I could go home as well. So that I could see my Father in person, curl up in His lap, lay my head on His shoulder, and have His arms around me as He tells me He loves me. He sent His Son to die—for me, for you, to make a way for us to return home to Him.

Jesus spent a short time here, but before He could return home, He went through Hell. Jesus experienced everything that we do in His short time here. His path wasn't easy. Those He loved and trusted broke His heart—when they lied, when they turned their backs on Him, when they sold Him out for money. Others stood fast but were heartbroken because they didn't fully understand what He was doing. My Big Brother, Jesus, died an unimaginably horrible death—for me. For you. It was brutal. Then, He went to Hell for three days—so that we don't have to.

THAT is love.

THAT is the ultimate Father and Brother.

Forgiveness? Really? What about anger? What about hurt? What about sorrow? Yeah, those all played a role, too. They came in waves. One day, it was the ache of loss—losing everything I thought I knew about my biological father. Losing his family. Losing my identity to a degree. Then came the anger. I had always believed everything my mom told me. Always. I never imagined she would lie to me, and certainly not about something this huge. Because it *was* huge. Earth-shakingly huge. And then, the hurt. Boy, did it hurt.

As a small child, I never knew the man who I believed to be my biological father. He was never in the picture. Mom left him when I was only six months old. There was limited contact as I grew up— extremely limited contact. Child support checks once a month. I received a Raggedy Ann and Andy music box that played *This Old Man* after I had been in the hospital for a week. A few phone calls here and there and limited visits over a decade until his death. That was it.

Even though Dad came into my life when I was young and was a wonderful father, I still desperately wanted to know who my biological father was. I craved that knowledge.

There was a gaping hole where that desire originated. I had so many questions. Wouldn't you?

Maybe not. But I sure did.

I got my answers when I met him. I got to know Allen—the type of man he was—and finally, I was so thankful for the dad who raised me. It was great finally getting my answers and getting to know Allen. But the true gift in meeting him was Lola.

Through it all, the love of the Lord showed on her face, in her eyes, in her smile. She glowed. She loved me. She welcomed me with open arms. She was so dainty and frail in body—but in spirit? She was a mighty warrior. And pray? Boy, could she pray!

Lola was a wonderful blessing, and I'm so grateful I got to have her as my great-grandmother, even if only for a short time. Losing her was hard enough, but when I discovered that Allen wasn't my father, it felt like I lost her all over again. Even though, in reality, that loss was only in name—she had already passed away in November 1996.

Losing Lola was hard enough. But losing that Cherokee connection too was yet another fracture in the foundation of who I thought I was.

More loss.

The hole was back. The questions resurfaced.

None of the answers.

And just like that, the search began again.

Amid the search and the loss, I tried to forgive.

Some days? I felt like I had it in me.

Other days? I was angry, hurt, and drowning in the struggle.

This was big.

Huge, even.

I remember standing at the kitchen island, trying to cook—and completely losing it.

Music has always been my comfort, my refuge. I almost always have it playing in the house, filling the spaces where silence feels too heavy. That day, "Thy Will" by Hillary Scott & The Scott Family came on.

And the longer it played, the harder my heart ached.

Tears burned my eyes. The lyrics sank in, cutting deep, exposing every raw place I had tried to push aside. I started singing along, my voice shaky, breaking.

And with every "*Thy will be done*"—I stomped my foot.

Hard.

It wasn't just a song anymore. It was a battle cry. A plea. A surrender I didn't know how to give.

So, I put it on repeat.

And for the next fifteen minutes, I cried.

That moment was one of my turning points in this whole journey. By the time I was done—crying, singing, praying—I felt lighter. I had truly given it to God. And then, I could forgive.

Forgiveness is big. For many reasons. It's not just about the person you are forgiving. It's about you. Holding onto anger and pain? It only hurts you. Rarely does it affect the person you feel it toward. If you hold onto it for too long; you will become an angry, bitter person. And that is not who I wanted to be.

Now, don't get me wrong. I'm not perfect—not by any stretch of the imagination. So, yes—there were moments when the pain crept back in, when I had to forgive again. But those moments became fewer and farther between.

And today, eleven years later? I don't have to work on it anymore. It's solid. I have fully forgiven my mom. Looking back,

I couldn't tell you the exact moment when it happened, when I stopped sliding back into anger and hurt. I just know that today, I have truly let it go.

Take a minute. Who do you have in your life that you need to forgive? For whatever reason? Who just popped into your mind? That very first person? Now, take that person to God. Pray for them. Ask God to guide your steps, to help you release whatever anger you're holding, whatever it is that you need to forgive them for. It may take time. It may not happen all at once. Keep praying. Every time you see them. Every time you think of them. Pray. Pray for wisdom in how you treat them. Pray to see them as God sees them.

God can only forgive us if we forgive others. He tells us so. And beyond that? Forgiveness frees you. It lifts the weight, the burden, the heaviness you've been carrying. It changes you. So, I'm praying for you now.

> *God, be with the person reading this. As they pray for and forgive the person they need to forgive, help them. Show them how wonderful it will be to let go of the hurt, the anger, the pain. Thank You, Father, for all You do for us. Amen.*

Field Notes:
Evidence for Healing

Even when earthly fathers fail us, our Heavenly Father calls us His own.

REFLECTION QUESTIONS

- How has your view of God as Father changed over time?

- Have you ever wrestled with the idea that God is personal and deeply loving?

- What would it look like to let Him father you in the places you feel abandoned?

WRITING PROMPT

Write a letter or prayer to God as your Father. Be honest—share your hurts, your hopes, and what you're still learning about His love.

ENCOURAGEMENT

You are fully known and fully loved. God didn't miss a moment of your story. Where others left, He stayed. Where others were silent, He spoke. You are not fatherless. You are claimed, cherished, and carried by your Abba Father.

SCRIPTURE ANCHOR

"And when you stand praying, if you hold anything against anyone, forgive them, so that your Father in heaven may forgive you your sins." – **Mark 11:25**

PRAYER

Abba, You knew who I was long before I ever figured it out. Thank You for sticking with me through every wrong turn, every broken hope, every messy middle. When I doubt, remind me that I'm Yours—on my best days, my worst days, and every crazy, beautiful day in between. Help me to wear Your love like armor and walk like a daughter who knows exactly whose she is. Amen.

CASE FILE #013

Anchored in Hope: Finding Peace in God's Promises

"For you created my inmost being; you knit me together in my mother's womb. I praise you because I am fearfully and wonderfully made; your works are wonderful, I know that full well. My frame was not hidden from you when I was made in the secret place. When I was woven together in the depths of the earth."
– Psalm 139:13-15

"Yes, my soul, find rest in God; my hope comes from him."
– Psalm 62:5

Hope.

It's such a small word, but it carries the weight of the world. And in God, hope isn't fleeting or fragile—it's a foundation, a lifeline, an anchor that steadies us in the fiercest storms. Looking back, I see how hope carried me when I thought I couldn't take another step. I see how God's promises held me steady when everything else felt like it was crumbling. His love has been my constant, even when I didn't realize it, even when I doubted it. There is always hope in God. No matter what.

He knows us. Long before we are even a thought. Before we are conceived, **God knows us**. He **loves us** and **sees us**. He knows the path He has laid out for us, as well as the paths and choices we will make along the way.

There is always a way back to hope—even when we wander far from it. Hope that we will make the decisions that lead us closer to Him and His love. But even when we stumble and make choices that lead us down paths of pain, there is hope that we will find our way. Find our way to Him. Where there is love, hope, and forgiveness.

Looking back on my journey, I can see God's fingerprints all over my story, even in the moments when I felt completely alone. It's clear that my journey has been a winding road—a mix of heartbreak, resilience, joy, and discovery. There were moments when I couldn't see the path ahead, moments when I thought I would never get answers. But God was always there, holding me, guiding me, and weaving together a story far greater than I could have written myself.

I think back to the days when I was desperately searching, convinced that finding my biological father would somehow complete me. I was consumed by questions: Who am I? Where do I come from? Why didn't he stay? And yet, even when the answers felt out of reach, God was quietly working behind the scenes—orchestrating connections and filling the gaps with His love.

Throughout my journey, there were moments when hope felt like a flickering candle, barely enough to light my next step. But somehow, even in the darkest places, hope found me. His presence never left—steady and silent, even when I couldn't feel it. I think about the afternoon I sat in the chapel at Allen's funeral, clutching the folded flag presented to me for his military service. In my hands, I wasn't just holding a flag—I was holding a lifetime of unmet expectations, a tangled mix of love and anger, and the weight of everything I had lost. At the time, it felt like the end of the road—the weight of every unanswered question pressing down on me, making it one of the darkest moments of my life. And yet, even then, a whisper of hope flickered—a glimmer that reminded me I wasn't alone, that God still had more in store for me.

I remember standing at Lola's gravesite, pouring my heart out to the woman who welcomed me into her family without hesitation, even when she didn't have to. I thanked her for her love, for being the grandmother I didn't know I needed. In that quiet moment, speaking to a grave, I felt God's presence so tangibly. It was as if He were whispering, **"See? I've been here all along—filling the gaps, loving you through it all."** That moment wasn't just about saying goodbye to Lola; it was a profound reminder of how God had used her love to show me His own—steady and unshakable, even in the spaces where I felt most broken.

And then there was the retreat—where God met me in a way I'll never forget. The warmth of the oil flowing over me, the whispered words of encouragement from a woman who didn't know my story but somehow spoke directly to my heart. "Your answer is coming," she said. And it did—though not in the way I expected. God poured His oil over me, His promises whispered to my heart. He showed me that my answer was coming, and though I didn't know how or when, I chose to trust Him.

Hope has a funny way of sneaking up in the simplest places—in shared laughter, unexpected phone calls, or quiet nights with my Bible. I think about the laughter I shared with my aunt Elaine and my cousin Angie during those early days of getting to know my new family. We sat around the table swapping stories, filling in the gaps of years we hadn't shared. In those moments, I felt a deep sense of belonging I hadn't even realized I was missing. I think about the unexpected phone call from Eric, the excitement in his voice as we talked about the possibility of being siblings. Even though that particular thread didn't lead to the answers I was looking for, it reminded me that every connection is a gift, every step forward is a part of the journey. And I think about the nights I spent alone with my Bible, pouring out my heart to God, asking for guidance and clarity. Those quiet moments, where it was just me and Him, were some of the most transformative. It wasn't just about finding my father—it was about finding myself in Him.

When I discovered—yet again—that I didn't know the truth about my birth father, something shifted. This moment marked a turning point in my relationship with God—or at least with this part of my life. I realized that no matter what happened, no matter who my earthly father was or wasn't, God had always been there. He is my Father. The One who never left, never abandoned me, never stopped loving me and never would. In Him, I found a love so complete, so steady, that it filled the cracks left by every human failure.

His promises fill my heart when the ache tries to creep back in. His truth is the foundation I now stand on. And His faithfulness is my anchor, holding me steady no matter how fierce the storms of life become. I've come to understand that He'll never let me fall—not truly. Even in moments when I felt broken, He was always there, picking up the pieces, reshaping them into something beautiful.

I chose to believe in His plan, even when I couldn't see it. I chose to trust that all the pain, all the waiting, all the unanswered questions had a purpose. Not because it's easy, but because He's shown me time and again that His ways are perfect, even when they don't make sense to me.

This part of my journey has taught me that healing doesn't always come the way we expect it to. Sometimes, it comes not through answers but through surrender. It comes in letting go of what we think we need and trusting in the One who already knows. The pain may have shaped me, but it doesn't define me. God does. His love does.

And as I stand here, reflecting on the winding, messy, beautiful path that brought me to this moment, I know one thing for certain: I am His. And that's more than enough.

As I write these final words, I want to turn the focus to you. This isn't just my story—it's a shared experience of searching, longing, finding, and holding onto hope.

Now it's your turn.

What anchors you? What are the moments, the people, the experiences that have held you steady in the storm? I invite you to take a deep breath, pause, and reflect.

Write a Letter to God. Start with something as simple as a pen and paper. Write to Him about where you are right now—your joys, your hurts, your questions, and your dreams. Tell Him what you're holding onto and what you're ready to surrender. Writing it down can bring clarity and draw you closer to Him.

Reflect on Your Own Journey. Think back on the moments that shaped you—the highs, the lows, the unexpected twists. How did they bring you to where you are today? Write them down or share them with someone close to you. Sometimes, just speaking your story out loud can bring healing and perspective.

Identify Your Anchors. Who or what has helped you through hard times? Is it a friend, a family member, a mentor, or your faith? Acknowledge their impact, thank them, and lean into those sources of strength.

Take a Step toward Healing. If there's someone you need to forgive—whether it's a family member, a friend, or even yourself—start that process today. It doesn't have to be perfect, and it doesn't have to be immediate. But taking that first step can begin to set you free.

Spend Time in Scripture. God's Word is full of promises that remind us of His love and faithfulness. Take a few moments to read verses that speak to you about hope, healing, and belonging. Start with **Jeremiah 29:11, Isaiah 40:31, or Psalm 46:1.** Let His words settle in your heart.

Connect with Community. Don't go it alone. Whether it's a church, a small group, or a trusted friend, find people who can walk alongside you. Share your heart with them and let them share theirs with you. Together, you can encourage one another to stay anchored in hope.

Pray with Expectation. Whatever is on your heart right now, bring it to God in prayer. Trust that He hears you, sees you, and will answer in His perfect timing. It may not look like what you expect, but it will always be what you need.

Hope is never lost when it is placed in God.

No matter where you are in your journey, no matter what questions still linger, know this:

You are seen, you are loved, and you are never alone.

Whatever you're facing, wherever you are, *you are not alone.* God sees you. He knows you. He loves you. And He's been with you every step of the way, even when it didn't feel like it. Your journey is unique, and so is your hope. Hold onto it tightly. Let it carry you through the storms and bring you back to calm waters. Trust that God is using every piece of your story to create something beautiful—something only He can see right now. When you look back, I hope you'll see, as I have, that God was there all along—guiding, loving, and anchoring you in His unshakable hope.

God is always there, holding us, guiding us, even when we can't see it. He takes our broken pieces and turns them into something beautiful. He fills the gaps, heals the wounds, and gives us a hope that is unshakable.

No matter where you are on your journey, **remember this:** With God, there is always hope. Hope that anchors us. Hope that steadies us. Hope that carries us forward into a future we can't yet imagine.

And so, I leave you with this: **Trust Him. Seek Him. Let Him be your anchor. The God Who Never Fails**

Because the God who knows you, who loves you, who has been with you every step of the way, will never fail you.

Throughout this book, I've shared moments that felt like the end of the world—the lies, the losses, the long periods of waiting. But I've also shared moments where God's love broke through, shining like a beacon in the storm. These moments remind me of one of my favorite scriptures:

> *"We have this hope as an anchor for the soul, firm and secure."* (Hebrews 6:19a)

I think about the vision God gave to the woman at the retreat, showing me surrounded by boulders and gushing water, yet held steady in His lap. At the time, I didn't fully understand it, but now I see how it reflects the way He's carried me through every trial. Even when I felt like I was drowning, He was there, holding me close.

I think about the laughter I shared with my newfound family members, the tears shed over the graves of loved ones I never had the chance to meet, and the peace I found in moments of forgiveness. Each of these experiences was a reminder that God's plan is greater than my pain.

If you're reading this, it's likely because you're on your own journey—a quest for answers, for healing, or maybe just for a little hope. Let me tell you this: You are not alone.

God sees you. He hears you. And even in the darkest moments, He is there, weaving a story of love and redemption in your life. You may not see it now—you may not even believe it—but I promise, His plan for you is beautiful. Hold on to that hope.

I've learned that hope doesn't mean everything will be easy or that the pain will disappear overnight. It doesn't mean every question will be answered in the way you expect. But hope does mean that there is always a reason to keep going. It means trusting that even in the hardest times, God is working all things together for good.

As I write these final words, I'm struck by how much my journey has shaped me. It hasn't been easy—there were days when I wanted to give up, when the weight of it all felt unbearable. But those days taught me something invaluable: God's love is steadfast. His hope is unshakable. And His plan is always worth trusting.

To anyone who feels like they've lost their anchor, I encourage you to reach out to Him. Let Him steady you in the storm. Let Him guide you back to the path He has prepared for you. And above all, let Him fill you with hope—a hope that will carry you through whatever lies ahead.

With God, hope never fails. It anchors us–even when everything else feels adrift.

Field Notes:
Evidence for Healing

Hope isn't based on the outcome of our search, it's anchored in the One we find.

REFLECTION QUESTIONS

- What has hope looked like in your life—in the best moments, and in the hardest ones?

- When have you felt like giving up, and what (or who) helped you keep going?

- What would it look like to anchor your identity in God, no matter your earthly story?

ENCOURAGEMENT

Hope isn't wishful thinking—it's holy defiance. It's standing in the storm and saying, "I still believe." Even when things don't make sense. Even when healing is slow. You are not forgotten. You are not lost. You are anchored in something stronger than grief, fear, or rejection. You are anchored in Him.

WRITING PROMPT

Describe a moment you felt hopeless. Then write about the person, scripture, or whisper from God that helped you hold on. What changed in you because you chose to stay anchored?

SCRIPTURE ANCHOR

"We have this hope as an anchor for the soul, firm and secure." – **Hebrews 6:19a**

PRAYER

Lord, when the waves rise and the storms roar, anchor my heart in You. Remind me that hope is not wishful thinking—it's the steady, unshakable trust that You are who You say You are. When I can't see the shore, teach me to hold fast to Your promises. Let my life be tethered not to circumstances, but to Your unchanging love. Amen.

Final Report: Case Closed (But Never Forgotten)

"I will not leave you as orphans; I will come to you."
– John 14:18

Investigation complete. Truth uncovered. Identity secured. Case closed—with love.

After years of searching, countless clues, dead ends, and divine revelations, the case is closed—not because I found every answer I thought I needed, but because I found the One answer that mattered most.

I searched for a father.

I found three. I uncovered secrets, lost identities, shattered illusions, and surprising new beginnings.

But above all—I found truth.

And that truth wasn't hidden in DNA reports, courthouse documents, or family trees. It was found in the relentless, unwavering love of a Father who never once left me.

This file—**The Daddy Files**—was never really about *them*.

It was about *me*.

And it was about *God*.

How He pursued me. How He held me. How He named me. How He redeemed every broken thread woven into my story.

He turned my investigation into a testimony. He turned ashes into beauty. He turned abandonment into belonging.

This journey was messy. It was complicated. It was often painful. But it was also holy.

Because through it all—through every lost lead, closed door, whispered prayer, and sleepless night—I was seen. I was known.

I was fiercely loved.

By the One who didn't need a blood test to claim me. By the One who had called me *His* from the very beginning.

I thought I was chasing earthly answers. In reality, I was chasing belonging—and it was waiting for me all along.

Identity was never about biology. It was about being known, loved, and chosen.

The missing pieces weren't missing after all. They were being held safely in the hands of a God who makes everything beautiful in its time.

If you're still searching—whether for identity, healing, or hope—know this:

You are not forgotten. You are not lost. You are not too broken.

There is a Father who knows your true name. He has never misplaced you. He has never once left your side.

May you find the courage to keep asking the hard questions, the grace to heal from the hard answers, and the faith to trust that the best parts of your story are still being written.

And the Author? He writes with love.

Field Notes:
Evidence for Healing

Closure doesn't mean forgetting—it means moving forward with truth, healed and whole.

REFLECTION QUESTIONS

- What verdict would you write about your own journey right now?

- What did you learn about yourself that surprised you?

- What would you say to the version of you who started the search?

ENCOURAGEMENT

God finishes what He starts. No loose ends. No wasted pain. Every thread in your story has purpose—even the ones you wish had been written differently. There's healing in the naming. There's strength in the searching. And there's wholeness in Him.

WRITING PROMPT

Write your own "final report." What's the case you've been trying to solve in your life? What have you uncovered? What are you still waiting to discover?

SCRIPTURE ANCHOR

"And we know that in all things God works for the good of those who love him, who have been called according to his purpose." – **Romans 8:28**

PRAYER

Father God, You are the beginning, the middle, and the end of my story. When others left question marks over my life, You wrote Your name over everyone. You saw every missing piece, every broken dream, and You called me Yours anyway. Thank You for chasing me down, for holding me up, and for speaking truth louder than the lies. Help me walk forward, head high, heart steady—anchored not in what I lost, but in the love I can never lose. You are my Abba Father. That is the only answer I'll ever truly need. In the mighty name of Jesus, Amen.

Addendum to the Case: Reopened, Reviewed ... and Reconciled

Every investigator knows that even after the case is closed, there's always a little more to the story. And this one—my story—wouldn't be complete without an honest update about my mom and me.

Growing up, my mom was my best friend. We were close in the way some daughters only dream of—we talked daily, took trips together, and shared just about everything. But when the truth came to light—the secret she had carried for decades—our bond took a hit. A hard one.

We went through a season where we didn't talk at all. The silence between us felt heavier than the lies. For the first time in my life, I didn't know how to reach her ... and she didn't know how to reach me.

But healing, like detective work, takes time. Clues come slowly. Breakthroughs happen in quiet moments. And over time, we began to rebuild. Through prayer, hard conversations, and a whole lot of grace, our relationship was restored.

In fact, when I wrote my chapter for a collaborative book called *Anchored in Hope*—a story about the season when we thought my young son had leukemia and how God walked me through both that fear and the process of forgiving my mom—she read it. We talked. We cried. And I told her, out loud and without hesitation, that I had forgiven her.

She's read this book, every word. And she gave it her blessing. Not because it's easy to read, but because we both believe someone else might find hope and healing in these pages.

So yes, this case is still personal. But now it's also a testimony. Not just of family secrets and DNA surprises—but of restoration, forgiveness, and the God who's never once stopped pursuing us.

From Me to You:

If you're holding a broken relationship in your hands right now—one that feels too far gone, too complicated, or too painful to revisit—I want you to know: it's not over. God can work in the messiest places. He can soften hearts, restore what feels shattered, and bring healing where there's been silence.

Keep praying. Keep showing up. Keep hoping.

You never know what can happen when grace steps into the story.

Scripture:

"I will repay you for the years the locusts have eaten ..." – Joel 2:25

"Sometimes the hardest stories to tell are the ones that offer the most healing—especially when grace has the final word." – Melissa Jean Rod

www.ingramcontent.com/pod-product-compliance
Lightning Source LLC
Chambersburg PA
CBHW031504120626
46545CB00005B/1748